LEAP, DON'T SLEEP!

**How to get different
results by doing some-
thing different**

JOHN MADDEN

LDS Publishers
2542 Winstead Circle
Wichita, KS 67226

ORDERING INFORMATION
Special discounts are available on quantity purchases by corporations, associations, and others. For details, contact the publisher at the address above. For individual sales, visit
www.LeapDontSleep.com.

Printed in the United States of America by ADR Bookprint, Inc.
Cover and layout by Susan Sellers

ISBN: 0-9720645-0-8

Library of Congress Control Number: 2002091736

CONTENTS

DEDICATION

This book is dedicated to everyone who has ever attended one of my lectures or seminars, and nodded your head with understanding, asked a question which made me be prepared, and laughed when I was supposed to be humorous. It is to all my clients, friends, and family from whom I have always learned something, and whose encouragement has led me to the words and ideas I share in this book.

ACKNOWLEDGEMENTS

I am most grateful to the following people who helped in some way to make this book possible:

Charlotte Patterson, who asked me to present a different kind of talk to her association members, resulting in the creation of Leap, Don't Sleep!

Karen Anderson, Toni Raines, and **Beth Young** — Editors.

Doug Smart, who presented a great workshop on getting published to my NSA (National Speakers Association) chapter in Kansas City.

Penny Burgess, author of *Penny's Diner*.

Gordon Kessler, author of *Jezebel*.

Paul Khouri and **Rod Jones** of Yia Yia's Eurobistro restaurants, whose dedication to service excellence gave me great examples.

INTRODUCTION

We cannot become what we want to be by remaining what we are.

— SOCRATES

Today, we're in a radically changing world — where competition is becoming more global and fiercer. Work demands are greater, and companies of all sizes are re-structuring, downsizing, and outsourcing. We're having to change the way we operate. We're expected to produce at a much faster pace than we're used to. We're overwhelmed by information about new products and services, new technology, and new ways of doing business. We're being dragged forcibly through an era of super high-tech and super high stress.

How can we survive all this change and come out ahead? This is the question on the minds of most people in business today. But there is a small number of people out there who know that they can't stand still, who know that in order to survive and succeed they have to change two things: their thinking and their actions. Stephen Covey, in *The Seven Habits of Highly Effective People*, tells us we have to change our paradigms, the way we see things, the way we see the world. We tend to see the world as we are, not as the world is.

We're uncomfortable with change, so we resist it. And we try to hold onto old habits, which are not advancing us, let alone helping us to keep up. We work harder and harder doing the same old thing, hoping for a different result. Some call this insanity! A much-used phrase, "If you keep doing what you've always done, you'll always get what you've always got," appears to make sense more than ever.

So what's the answer? How do we move from where we are to where we want to be? We obviously have to *take action*, but what action? There's so much happening, we say, it's hard to know where to start!

Well, you need a map, don't you? How else will you know where you're going, or if you're getting there? My map — or guide — is called "Leap, Don't Sleep." *How to get different results by doing something different.* It's a wake-up call to the brain, a step-by-step guide to changing the results you're getting in your business, your job, and in your life — to the results you want, and the results you're capable of achieving.

"Leap, Don't Sleep" is an acronym with each letter carrying an important message, which will be easy to remember. You can incorporate this into your management or functional responsibilities, and into your everyday life. You can adapt it to train and educate others to be creative, productive, and successful. You can immediately impact and accelerate the profit growth of your company by better serving your external paying customers, and your internal resource customers — your employees and co-workers. We'll start with the letter "L": "Look for a better way."

CHAPTER 1

L
LOOK FOR A
BETTER WAY

If you want to change the future, you must change what you're doing in the present.

— MARK TWAIN

We cannot solve today's problems with old-fashioned remedies. You wouldn't run a word-processing business with an old IBM typewriter, would you? Of course not! You might eventually get the job done, but you won't be competitive. Or, if you're in the business of carpentry or renovating people's houses, you won't be a great financial success, nor will you make much money if you're still using non-power tools. There are examples all around us of people using innovative ways of doing things; creative and revolutionary ways of solving problems and becoming more competitive in business; and breaking old rules to set new standards of accomplishment in meeting customers' needs in quality, speed, and value, while saving time and money.

A few years ago Robert Kriegel wrote the book *If It Ain't Broke, Break It!* He takes a hard look at the traditional resistance to change, and encourages us to "mess with success.", to get out of our comfort zones and to adapt "break-it thinking." This is a good reference for examining *conventional* versus *unconventional wisdom.*

We've all moved along at varying speeds, as we became part of the world of the Internet, e-mail, and the cell phone. While there is the inevitable discontent and frustration with some technological advances — such as the impersonal feeling of listening to pre-recorded voice systems that you can't talk back to — and computers that sometimes crash, leaving you helpless, we have moved a long way at break-neck speed. We have, for the most part, progressed far more than we give ourselves credit. The real challenge is how do we keep up?

What it boils down to is that we have to find ways, not only to keep pace with what's happening around us, but also to take advantage of the opportunities available to advance way beyond where we are right now.

I, myself, had to do some serious catching-up. I started my own speaking business at the age of 54, having never worked on a computer, hardly ever made sales calls, or compiled financial statements. I'd had the luxury of an administrative assistant or secretary for most of my management career. I struggled for the first year with low-tech habits that qualified me as the novice business owner I'd become. I surely had to find a better way to run my business — if only to gain some credibility as a competent professional.

In the corporate world, I was able to do my job quite adequately with the assistance of a shared administrative assistant, weekly and monthly financial reports, inter-office communications, and faxes. When I started my own business, I hired an assistant on a call-in basis to do my letters and invoicing. This was not always economical — or practical — as she was rarely available when I needed her, and never on weekends. So I found myself writing out letters, proposals, and lectures, in longhand for her to tackle on her home computer when she could work it in.

Later I splurged on a $350 word processor and elimi-nated the call-in person, except for when I needed real fancy stuff that my word processor couldn't do. Of course I soon realized that the quality of work produced on the word processor looked little better than that from an old electric typewriter. I did not feel that I was putting out a great image as a professional. As I later mingled with sea-soned speakers and trainers through the association lunch-eons and get-togethers, I realized painfully that I had much to do to get up to speed. I exhausted the good nature of a friend who managed a jewelry store when he told me he could no longer accept faxes for me on his machine. So the fax machine was my next capital investment.

I also found myself embarrassed talking on the phone to potential clients when my call waiting would kick in. The call was often for another member of the family, and even if I ignored it, the client appeared to be easily dis-tracted by it. So I put in voice-mail and got rid of call waiting and the answering machine.

In my second year of business I bought a used laptop from my first computer mentor, a fellow speaker and marketing advisor, Ford Saeks, who forcibly dragged me up to speed. I was so nervous in the beginning that I called him all hours of the day and night with "problems." After a while he stopped returning my calls — his gentle way of telling me to read the manual, to practice, and to figure it out for myself. It was the best thing he could've done for both of us.

Perhaps you can relate in some small way to my experiences here. However, my point is that we all have some changes in our lives, and we have to deal with them in order to move forward, to be successful, and to survive. In short, if we want different results, we have to do something different. And change is not going to stop: it's as inevitable as death and taxes, and more so every day! We have to keep up. We have to stay current. We have to be prepared to compete in a radically changing world. We have to look for better ways of solving problems, better ways of doing business, better ways of communicating, better ways of getting along, and especially better ways of handling stress while dealing with all the bigger demands on our time and our life.

What is it that you have to gain by finding a better way?

Look at it this way, what problems do you have in your job, your business, or your life that are crying out for solutions? Are you trying to make more money — struggling to pay off your credit card? Are you having trouble getting along with your boss, with a difficult customer, or a family member? Would you like to spend fewer hours at the office? Are you frustrated in your efforts to get your employees self-motivated?

What have you been doing to solve these problems? What results, if any, have you had? Are you satisfied? If not, what have you done differently to get a different result? Have you just given up? Then you're not the exception, you're the average! And if you're average, your results are likely to be mediocre.

Exceptional or above-average people are always looking for a better way, a new invention, a revolutionary breakthrough, and ultimately they get it. What do they gain? Progress, prestige, the satisfaction of achievement, the knowledge that they tried even if it didn't happen that time, a sense of contribution, the thrill of making a difference. The following is an example of a teamwork effort to find a solution to an annoying problem for hotel guests and for hotel desk clerks.

In a brainstorming session with a client who owns some hotels, we found out from the front desk employees of a recently opened hotel that many guests — particularly the elderly — had difficulty opening their bedroom door with the electronic key card which is now commonplace. Often, in frustration, guests came down to the lobby to complain and request another room. The desk clerk usually tried to explain how the card key works, and sometimes even went to the guests' room to make sure they successfully entered the room. Can you imagine the inconvenience to the guest and the resulting frustration on the part of the employees who have to take the heat for this, again and again?

We needed an answer to this problem right here at the meeting. After some wild and creative ideas were thrown into the arena, the employees came up with several possible solutions — not all of which were workable — but from them we settled on what proved to be a most practical solution, and which, since then, has dramatically improved customer service and reduced the many guests' unnecessary frustrations.

The solution was to put a replica of the lock in an attractive wood casing at the front desk so that anyone could practice using the key card before going to the room. This cost little, but it had a huge impact on customer service. It demonstrated an interest on the part of the hotel to make life easier for its guests. Rather than allowing the problem to continue, they determined a way to resolve it. They looked for a *different way*.

You see, this kind of problem often goes unsolved because we think that the way we're handling it is all we can do, that it's the only *logical* thing to do in the circumstances. We decide to live with it. And the customer suffers. And if the customer suffers, the customer moves on to a non-suffering environment — to your competitor!

How do you go about finding a better way?
1. Look for the second right answer — and the third.
2. Draw on previous experience, knowledge, and contacts.
3. Brainstorm with others. Ask, "What if?" or "Why not?"

Look for the second right answer

Too often we come to the conclusion that the solution we're working with is the only logical solution there is, and that if it doesn't work, we just need to try harder so that we can say, "at least we tried"; or we just accept the status quo and hope that things will get better somehow.

Consider this: is aspirin the only way to cure a headache? Of course not, although it is for many the first right answer, and from our learning experiences at school, that there is only one right answer — some of us might consider it the only solution, and thereby suffer in silence if there isn't an aspirin available when we need one. In brainstorming with a class one day on other possibilities to cure a headache, we came up with over twenty alternatives, including the following: lie down; do yoga; drink herbal tea; put a cold compress on your forehead; if driving, open the window to get a cool breeze against your face; take a leisurely walk; put on soft music; get a massage; and so on.

I consulted for a manufacturing company who had high employee turnover and wanted me to help them correct this costly problem. I asked their human resource director what efforts had been made up till now to reduce turnover. She said, "We've tried everything, competitive pay and benefits, bonuses, free laundering of uniforms … you name it" I asked if they had any analysis on why people left the company. She brought me a huge pile of completed exit interview forms, which went back the last three years, but were not summarized in any way.

Having managed multiple operations, I had little faith in exit interviews due to the inevitable inaccuracy brought on by subjectivity and low confidentiality. I knew this analysis had minimum value. I asked her what percentage of the plant work force was stable. She told me 90 percent. So, only 10 percent of the workforce was turning over — a very important piece of information!

I suggested that rather than ask people who are leaving why they're leaving, let's ask people who stay why they stay.

We adapted an employee survey form, which I had worked with before. It was to be filled out by all employees. This asked twenty questions related to the following: work assignments, individual goals, availability of opportunities, recognition of accomplishments by supervisor, employee input to decision making, safety issues, direction of company, recommendations for operational improvement, and employee concerns. The forms were confidential, and not seen at first by anyone's direct supervisor (although the results were reviewed later with each supervisor). The employee's name did not have to appear, but they were asked to fill in the department in which they worked.

One interesting bit of information we found was that new people had a tough time fitting in to a fairly tight group of long-time workers. This problem had not been picked up on the exit interviews, although some of the comments made might cause one to wonder about the effectiveness of the orientation program.

The point here is that we began to make new progress in finding a solution by looking for another way to study the problem. It was always assumed that the only way to study turnover was to conduct exit interviews. We looked for a second right answer and found something different to try. But don't forget that sometimes the second right answer might not work — nor the third! You have to keep looking. Just consider all the right answers that didn't work before Edison finally invented the light bulb.

Draw on previous experience — Make a connection

The solution to a problem is usually found by combining something you know with something you don't know. Ralph Caplan, design critic, said, "All art and most knowledge entails either seeing connections or making them. Until it is hooked up with what you already know, nothing can ever be learned or assimilated."

For example, my wife and I were getting very frustrated with the toilet flush in one of our bathrooms, which used to disconnect from the link at the base of the cistern every second or third use. Whichever one of us was present when it disconnected usually fixed it by re-attaching it, hoping it would hold longer each time.

One day, thinking I should practice what I preach and look for a better way of solving this problem once and for all, I got a brainwave as I was throwing a twist-tie from my English muffins into the drawer. I went to the bathroom and flushed the toilet; and sure enough the chain unhooked from the link at the base, preventing the tank from filling. I hooked the chain and simply tied the twist-tie around it in the link, thus closing off the gap in the link and preventing the chain from separating. That was a year ago as I write this story, and the twist tie is still there although its original red color has faded. The chain has never come unhooked since that time.

The connection was made by considering the useful-
ness of something I was familiar with and applying it to a
different circumstance or problem. Historically, we can
see how more dramatic examples of this principle have
been used in creative inventions and product development.
For example, Gutenberg (considered by many to be the
most influential person of the last millennium) connected
the idea of the coin punch and the wine press to invent the
printing press. Fred Smith connected the airlines "hub and
spoke" distribution idea with that of an overnight package
delivery service to create Federal Express

Brainstorm with others. Ask "What if?" and "Why not?"

The collective intelligence of two or more people
gathered to solve a problem is much greater than the sum
of their individual efforts. It's all about *synergy* — and it
works like magic!

Get yourself a flip chart and some markers if you have
regular meetings with two or more people. This will be the
best fifty bucks, or thirty something pounds you'll ever
spend on creative thinking. The idea is to get a group-
focus on the problem. Everyone can see all the options
together. Write down every possible solution that is
offered, no matter how ridiculous or weird anyone thinks
it is.

It is from these brainstorming sessions that creative
ideas and solutions are born. This should be fun, with an
open mind and a sense of humorous exploration. Every
now and then one idea will spark another. Connecting one

idea with another concept or thought is often the beginning of an invention, as seen with the printing press, Velcro, the Post-It note, the Federal Express distribution system, and many others.

Ask, *What if?* and *Why not?* Allow any comical or off-the-wall answers to come into your mind. For extra stimulation, read *A Whack On The Side Of The Head* by Roger Von Oeck.

Here are some great things that have happened at the end of our last century. These things never would have occurred if someone hadn't asked, *What if?* or *Why not?* See how you can apply this thinking to the answers you hope to find for your project or for a problem you desperately need to solve. Do you remember these?

- *What if we could transplant a human hand?* This was first performed in France in 1998.
- *Why not bring back school uniforms?* Several states have brought back uniforms in schools and made dramatic reductions in juvenile crimes.
- *What if we invented a pill to cure impotence?* Viagra is often prescribed.
- *What if we could carry around a tiny phone in our purse or pocket?* The cell phone gets smaller each year.
- *Why not play golf at night?* The "glow-owl" golf ball was invented.
- *What if we had a pill to boost memory?* This is under development. I can't remember when they said it would be ready!

RECAP

1. Look for the second right answer — and the third.
2. Draw on previous experience, knowledge, and contacts.
3. Brainstorm with others. Ask, "What If?" and "Why not?"

Application Exercise

Write down:

1. What problem(s) have you been unsuccessful in solving?
2. What solutions have you tried in order to solve the problem?
3. What might be another way, a second right answer?
4. DO IT NOW! TRY IT!

CHAPTER

2

E
(CHANGE YOUR)
EXPECTATIONS

*You cannot tailor-make the situations in life,
but you can tailor-make your attitude to fit
those situations.*

— ZIG ZIGLAR

A s we go about trying to improve or change the status quo, and as we use the techniques of looking for a better way, we will find obstacles along the way, sometimes just a few, sometimes a lot. But if we are pursuing a lofty goal, the chances are that nothing will come easily. Recognizing this fact is crucial if we're to start off right. We need an air of persistence to add to our enthusiasm and our belief in the project we're undertaking.

You've heard the expression, "It's all in the mind." That usually refers to how we feel about certain things, problems, challenges, people, and situations. As we try new things, even with enthusiasm, there's often a conflict between what we know to be the right thing to do and our gut instinct to resist it. There's an expectation or a presumption that everything should be easy, and that we should continue to be comfortable. We do seem to need our comfort zones.

So, when we confront a new approach or concept, whether desired or imposed, we subconsciously compare it to what we know or what we're used to — our frame of reference, our experience. For example, I became a contract speaker with a large seminar company after many years managing multiple hotels and restaurants. It was quite alien for me to be told what to do by people far younger than I am. This was tough to take, even though I knew I was in a different environment, which would eventually lead to great things. I had to change my expectations. I had to realize that in this new business I'd gotten into, I was a novice, despite that in my preceding career I saw myself as an accomplished success.

Later, when I hired a person to type for me, I realized that her standards of reliability fell somewhat short of what I was used to in a secretary. She didn't have to work for me, and she didn't have the same sense of urgency that I had when important things had to be done. She had much greater priorities, family, children at school, and volunteering at the local church. What was important to me did not have the same significance to her. I had to adapt if I was to continue to use her services.

Our expectations can get us into a lot of trouble: our expectations of our company or our boss, our expectations of other people, even our expectations of ourselves. Someone said, "In life, a lot of things happen to us along the way." The truth is, we happen to a lot of things along the way. The impact of what happens to us is not caused by the event itself, but rather by how we see it. And how we see it is determined by how we feel about it. And how we feel about it is determined by what we think about it. And what we think about it is a choice we make, usually based on experience and perception.

What are your expectations of your company?

If you started working in the middle of the last century, your expectation was that you would spend most of your life with the same company, that they would take care of you as long as you showed up to work and did an average job. You would have a cost-of-living increase and a paid vacation every year, health insurance, a sick day and birthday allowance in many cases, and finally a pension to look forward to. This has all changed. It doesn't work like that anymore. Our 21st century global economy dictates that in business, we must be more competitive in quality, cost and delivery time. You are paid on performance, your individual performance. Just as your company is known by its brand name, now you are measured by your own accomplishments. Read Tom Peters' book, *Brand You*.

We have a new responsibility, to be a producer of results; and this is a dramatic change for most people. No more being carried, no more letting others do the real work while you just coast by. It requires a changed mindset. It's the big alert! And so, we must know and believe that we are capable of much greater things than we give ourselves credit. We must take some risks: that's the only way we'll learn how much more we can handle.

What are your expectations of other people?

In too many cases, our expectation of others needs to change. If we expect people to agree with us all the time, we're going to be very disappointed; we're also going to be inhibited in our communications with them, especially when it comes to brainstorming. After all, what's the point of brainstorming new ideas or solutions if different points of view are not explored?

We also have negative expectations about how some people — say, a new employee — will perform on the job. This may be based on their demeanor, their dress, their culture or any other factor. When I was facilitating a workshop with some fast-food restaurant managers, we were discussing the problem of employee turnover. I asked the group to list all the reasons they could think of why employees were absent, or didn't hold down a job for long. One of the reasons echoed by many of the managers was, "A lot of these people don't want to work." These managers really believed this to be true. In part of my response, I quoted something said by the then CEO of Cessna Aircraft Company, Russ Meyer, "Most people come to work to do a good job." I think part of the problem with some of the managers was that they had little time to train their new employees, and further, they had had almost no training in supervising and coaching skills. As a result the employees had little cause for self-motivation.

In some instances the managers viewed some applicants who were obviously from disadvantaged families as "losers." Yet, when I asked how many had in the course of their career been able to convert someone who had all the signs of failure into a success, most of them could remember at least one occasion when they had achieved this. If we expect people to fail, the chances are we will subconsciously do everything to prove ourselves right. We'll tend not to delegate responsibility, or we'll make too-frequent checks on their work, or we won't include them in problem solving groups.

What are your expectations of yourself?

We have misguided expectations of ourselves much of the time, expectations of what we are or are not capable of. Mostly, we place limits on what we can accomplish, how far we can go. We pepper all our discussions and statements with the word "but." "I could be a great doctor, but I didn't have a wealthy family who could afford to send me to college" "I would have saved a lot more money, but I made some bad investments." "I would've made my sales target, but a lot of people just didn't call back." Somebody once said," If you argue for your limitations, they're yours." Many times we allow small inconveniences to validate our rationale for not advancing in our career or in accomplishing certain goals, and in this way we justify our inaction.

I remember a few years ago an elderly friend of ours visited from England and stayed a couple of weeks. This was a well-traveled lady who was something of a professional vacationer, who always met new friends as she traveled the world. She was always open to new places and unknown territory, usually traveling alone. And yet with all this accomplishment, she was fearful of using a microwave oven because she'd never used one and thought all the dials looked complicated. I had to encourage her to shed her fear and embarrassment and follow my instructions on how to use this simple device. Up till then she believed that she'd probably never get the hang of this technology. She had placed limits on her ability to learn what most people in the Western world have been using since they were children. Needless to say, she was quite excited when she found out how simple it was.

I suppose I had the same concerns about using a computer, particularly as I was a rather slow typist, and I thought, how will I ever remember all those maneuvers that I'd seen other people do with apparent break-neck speed?

How do we change our expectations?
1. Know what you want and what it takes.
2. Get a different perspective. Reframe the problem.
3. Reward every little progress you make.

Know what you want, and what it will take

Surveys tell us that over ninety five per cent of the population have no written goals. Most of us have vague, undefined goals, kind of like dreamy wish lists:

One day, I'd like to go to Hawaii for a vacation.

I could be head of this department.

I'd love to have my own house on a lake, and so on.

If these are written down and looked at daily, there's a focus, a concentration that becomes part of your mechanism of purposeful living. If not, you'll languish in the mediocrity of wishful thinking.

> *If you don't change the direction you're going, you're likely to end up where you're headed."*

— Chinese Proverb

In order for you to get started on your goals, you must have a real sense of how this will affect your life: how much money will you have to borrow or spend? How long will it take? Will it break into your social calendar or into the time you usually spend with friends or family? What luxuries will you have to give up for a while? What kinds of barriers or obstacles will you most likely have to deal with? Are you prepared to go through all these changes and disruptions in your life knowing that anything that's really worthwhile doesn't usually come easily?

Get a different perspective — reframe the problem

Know what it takes to get what you want. Be aware of the obstacles that you're likely to encounter. As someone said, "Everything is difficult before it becomes easy." So many of us have given up at the first sign of defeat, thinking this is not for me, this couldn't work, this is crazy. We have stepped out of the comfort zone and we're dying to get back. We're threatened by insecurity and the fear of failure — sometimes by the *fear of success*! A book you should read is *Feel the Fear and Do It Anyway* by Susan Jeffers, Ph.D.

Change your expectations and ask, "What if?" In this way you suspend assumptions and get into an imaginative frame of mind; in other words, you put your mind in "open" mode so that anything flows.

Imagine what you would have said, if you had a closed mind, when a fellow at NASA wanted to send 77-year old John Glen into space. Maybe something like this, "You've got to be kidding, he'd never pass the physical. What happens if he doesn't survive or something goes wrong? We can't take a risk like that with a National hero!"

Instead of asking *what if we could?*, you'd be asking *what if it doesn't work?*, a symptom of the closed and fearful mind. These are expectations we have to change if we are to derive the benefits and rewards from creating or embracing change.

Another way to change your expectations is to *reframe* the situation. For example, if you have a long traffic-laden drive to work every day, which you never look forward to, look at it in a different way. What's good about spending an hour in your car every morning going to work, and another hour coming home at night? How about all that extra time you have to review what projects you'll be working on? Your drive provides time to brainstorm ideas with yourself, time to do some creative thinking which is difficult at the office with all the distractions, an opportunity to explore alternative ideas and solutions to problems that may be affecting your performance or that of others at work. Or you may like to drop in a CD or cassette and listen to some upbeat music to get you energized for the day's challenges, or a motivational tape to feed your mind with positive encouragement.

What if your flight is delayed and you're stuck at the airport for an extra hour? How would you reframe that situation from being a big inconvenience? Think of all the things you could do in that time instead of bellyaching with fellow passengers about the incompetence of the airlines. You could enjoy yourself watching people, catch up on some of that reading material you stuffed into your briefcase, take a brisk walk through the airport (What other exercise do you get when you're traveling?), call a friend or loved one, or return a business call you've been too busy to return.

That's all re-framing, getting a different view of any situation, and in many cases taking advantage of opportunities presented. Get yourself used to the idea of thinking like that in advance so that when the situation presents itself, you're ready to roll.

Often when something unusual happens to us, especially something unfortunate like a tragedy, we get a new perspective on life in general. A television interviewer asked Dr. Beck Weathers who survived a Mount Everest expedition where several people died, if his life had changed much as a result of his ordeal and the trauma he went through before he was rescued. He replied that he now had a whole new perspective on life, especially regarding one member of his family. Before he started the expedition he was in conflict with his son who had decided not to attend the university, which Weathers had attended, and all his family before him. His son decided to attend a less-celebrated college, which his girlfriend was planning to attend. Weathers worried about this as he was on the climb, but when his life was saved, he saw the situation in a totally different way. Now he realized how insignificant the college issue was against the value of life and the love of family. By getting a different perspective and by re-framing unpleasant situations, we will be more directed toward our goals and less sidetracked by inconveniences or petty annoyances.

Reward every little progress you make

Whenever you've made even the slightest leap forward in conquering your fears, or when you have approached a recurring problem from a different perspective and you have begun to see the benefit of your action, give yourself a pat on the back, an ice cream, a chocolate bar, or something that represents a victory celebration. When you validate the significance of your effort, you are setting yourself up to succeed further, and you are demonstrating to yourself that you have flexibility and a willingness to adapt as you pursue your goals. And your success at coping with change in today's fast-paced world will be measured by one little accomplishment at a time.

RECAP
1. Know what you want and what it takes.
2. Get a different perspective. Reframe the situation.
3. Reward every little progress you make.

Application Exercise

Write down:
1. One or two expectations that cause you problems or stress.
2. How does this affect your mood and your ability to perform?
3. Reframe and see another point of view.
4. How will this benefit you overall?
5. DO IT NOW!

A
ADD VALUE

If you quit getting better, you'll soon stop being good.

— J.WILLARD MARRIOTT

As stated before, in order to get different results and achieve excellence, we have to change what we are doing or the way we're doing it. In the world of business, we have three things in common. We are all customers in that we buy products and services from other people. Second, we are all in customer service as we provide products and/or services to other people. And third, we all need customers: customers are the very lifeblood of our economic existence.

When it comes to customers, our greatest challenge is to make sure they come back and buy from us again and again. How can we guarantee that that will happen?

Understand that in today's global economy, loaded with options, customers are demanding that products and services be faster, better quality, and cheaper; so in order to be truly competitive we have to be more creative in finding and keeping customers, more disciplined in controlling our costs, and more responsive to customer problems. In short, we need to be better than average. We need to eliminate average, we need to kill mediocrity.

It has become more than obvious to most of us that customer service has sunk to an all-time low in recent years. High tech has brought us low touch. To recover the much-desired high touch for our customers we have to add value.

How do you add value?
1. Give something that wasn't expected.
2. Do something different and better than your competition.
3. Implement a customer service recovery program.

Give something that wasn't expected

The outstanding companies, whether they be huge organizations or small retail stores, are known by how they delight their customers and exceed expectations. A restaurant called Yia Yia's Eurobistro in Wichita, Kansas is a good example. On one of my early visits to the restaurant several years ago, I was sitting at the bar having a sandwich and a glass of wine. I spotted a flask-shaped bottle on one of the shelves, which had the name "Tullamore

Dew" (an Irish whiskey) on the label. I asked the bartender, Steve, if I could have a closer look at the bottle. He promptly brought it down from the shelf and placed it on the counter for me. I was surprised to see this Irish whiskey in Kansas, and I shared with the bartender that Tullamore, the town where this liquor was made, was just a stones throw from where I was born in Ireland, and what a bit of nostalgia this elegant bottle had brought me.

A month later when I was having lunch at the restaurant, Steve, the bartender appeared at my table and presented me with the now-empty Tullamore Dew bottle that he had saved for me. As you can imagine I was overwhelmed, and this has been my restaurant of choice ever since. Nothing mediocre about the service here. He certainly added value to my experience.

On another occasion I was dining at Yia Yia's with a friend. He was disappointed that they didn't have baked potatoes on the menu, and was about to change his mind about eating there. The server, Joe, picked up on this quickly and said, "Sir, if you don't mind a slight delay, I'll get you a baked potato." Joe got one of the waiters to drive down the street to a nearby restaurant and return with a hot baked potato.

One day I needed to pick up a prescription at Gessler's drug store, which I'd only used once before. It is about a fifteen-minute drive, so I called to check on their closing time. The man who answered said they will be closing in five minutes, but he would be happy to deliver my prescription on his way home a half-hour later. Guess where I now go for my drug-store purchases.

Do something different and better than your competition

I have stayed in some hotels that place apples at the front desk, a welcome sight when I'm on the road and I don't know where or I don't have time to find fresh fruit.

There's a hardware store I go to where they offer tips on installing whatever you buy from them if they have the slightest hint that you're not a "professional handyperson."

A new hair stylist I tried gave me a head massage after she cut my hair. She not only removes hair, but also reduces stress!

All these little touches separate those businesses from their competition, simply because they're adding value in a different way.

Implement a customer service recovery program

A client said to me: "Most days things seem to run smoothly; but whenever we have a customer complaint we seem to collapse. Where are we going wrong?" How you handle and solve customer concerns and complaints is a measure of your standing in the "excellent," "bad," or "mediocre" category of customer service. Many companies fit into the "mediocre" (average) category where *indifference* and *defensiveness* best describe their operation. Are you sure this is not you?

Recently I returned from a business trip and was not pleased to find that two books I'd ordered three weeks before had not yet arrived, despite a promise from the book vendor that they would be delivered in five days. I was naturally upset and called the book vendor's long distance number. While I firmly told the lady who answered the phone how unhappy I was about their failure to deliver, and how this had greatly inconvenienced my schedule, she interrupted me right in the middle with: "Just a minute sir, you'll have to talk to customer service."

I said, "I'm sorry I thought you worked there."

She said, "I do."

I said, "Oh, I see, but you're not in customer service?"

She said, "That's right."

I said, "Well, I guess you'd better put me through to customer service then."

She said, "They've gone for the day." I detected some sadistic pleasure in the sound of her voice.

Not wishing to deny her the opportunity to take charge of the situation, I said,

"What should I do?"

She said, "You'll have to call back tomorrow."

No customer service recovery here. Only indifference and buck-passing, the symptoms of a mediocre company that tolerates less than outstanding customer service. Do you think I still do business with those people? Certainly not. Not when their competitors are just dying to steal me away! Not when I have many other options!

Contrast that mediocre service with the response from an Internet carrier I used before getting cable. Once, during their changeover of equipment, I was unable to access the Internet or my e-mail on the weekend for over two hours, which was very unusual. When I eventually called the office on Monday to complain, the lady in charge,

Melody, was most apologetic, explained about the equipment change, told me what she was going to do, got back to me in fifteen minutes (as she promised) with an update, and when all was fixed, she gave me her home number in case this ever happened on the week end again. Wow!

And the *piece de resistance*, on my next bill the monthly charge was waived! So, what was the difference here? The first company didn't have a customer service recovery program or policy, even though they probably *think* they have, and even though their brochures and publicity tell us they're the best! The second company walked the talk, knew why they were in business, knew that the customer has many choices, and they had a system for customer service recovery, putting it right for the customer.

RECAP
1. Give something that wasn't expected.
2. Do something different and better than your competition.
3. Implement a customer service recovery program.

Application Exercise

Write down:

1. One or two things you could do in your business that would be a pleasant surprise for your customers.

2. How does your company's service differ from your competition in a way that is obvious to customers? If it's not different, what could you do to make it stand out?

3. Do you have a customer service recovery program? Does it cover all the problems that your employees have to handle? If not, or if you're unsure, ask them.

4. Make a list of things that could, and do, go wrong; show how they should be handled, and how to prevent them from recurring.

5. Give your people the tools to do the job — training, authority to make a decision, adequate equipment and materials, and information.

6. At staff meetings, get employees' input on what improvements you could make to procedures that affect their ability to perform.

(continued on next page)

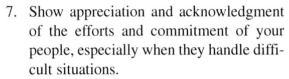

Application Exercise (continued)

7. Show appreciation and acknowledgment of the efforts and commitment of your people, especially when they handle difficult situations.
8. Call some of your customers who've had a problem and ask them how your company scored in service recovery!
9. DO IT NOW!

P

(BE) PROACTIVE, PLAN, PRIORITIZE

If you do the things you need to do when you need to do them, then you can do the things you want to do when you want to do them.

— ZIG ZIGLAR

Steven Covey in his *Seven Habits of Highly Effective People* says that to be proactive you must take responsibility for your actions and your attitude. Being proactive is being ready to respond effectively to events that will occur in the future. The old classic is the college final exams. If you studied and prepared through the year, you were in much better shape than the person who coasted and then spent the last night before the exam cramming.

Much of our failure in business and in life is caused by our habitual procrastination, putting off those actions that need to be taken if we are to advance further toward our goals. In my time management workshop called "Pull Yourself Together" we focus on the concept of *getting control* of your life, which really means being in charge and making choices that will cause you to be productive rather than passive.

Most people spend more time involved in activities rather than in action. I've been there many times. Writing this book is an example. When I first started, I had a tough time knuckling down and just writing. I spent too much time double-checking spelling, spacing and composition rather than just putting down all the ideas that came to me. Then I would get caught up reading more than I needed to in a reference source, thus distracting me from the job at hand.

We all know about the need to have specific goals and the need to plan in order to accomplish those goals. The problem is we get stuck in our daily routines, which make us feel comfortable and secure. The people who are visibly successful and making pots of money don't seem to have that problem. Why? Could it be that they really know what they want, that they are motivated by the knowledge that they are moving closer every day to that goal, and that they have chosen to control the inevitable distractions like television, spending too much time on the phone, partying late at night, reading trade magazines when they could be calling clients, and so on.

How can we be more proactive?
1. Read *The 15-Second Principle* by Al Secunda.
2. Understand the difference between *Urgent* and *Important*.
3. Learn how to say NO!

The 15-Second Principle
…by Al Secunda

Al Secunda wrote a book, which is a breakthrough in goal setting and goal achievement. The 15-second principle is designed to get us actively involved on our goals if only for 15 seconds a day.

I tried it myself on the first day I read it. As I write this piece, this is the twelfth consecutive day I've been writing. One day I wrote 750 words, another day I wrote only 22 words, but the discipline of opening up the file on the computer every day — no matter what — was what made it happen. I started on this book three years ago, picked it up again in September a year ago, and all I had written was 1500 words in two years. In the last twelve days I've added seven thousand words. Talk about being proactive!

Al Secunda's *The 15-Second Principle* acknowledges that we are for the most part poorly disciplined when it comes to managing our time and the accomplishment of our goals. We tend to see a single project in its entirety, and thus we see it as an awesome task. As a result we procrastinate again and again, hoping to find a bigger chunk of time to tackle this "beast." When we fail to knuckle down and do some part of the project, we make ourselves feel guilty and often abandon the project for a lengthy period of time, seeing it as being too hard to fit into our over flowing agendas. Al gets us to commit (on an agreement form) to spend a minimum of 15 seconds every day on some action to further our dream or goal.

He also tells us to promise to forgive ourselves if we fail any day to live up to our promise, but to recommit to the agreement the very next day. Having tried various forms of goal setting in the past, this method is working best for me as of this writing. My challenge now is to keep it up after the holidays when my business takes up more of my time. The only way I can convince myself to follow through with this routine is to recognize that this is part of my business. In fact, when I get this book in print I can have passive income. I can offer my book to my lecture and seminar attendees as a value-added marketing investment. Also, I can sell it on the Internet and in bookstores.

I have no problem turning on the computer and opening the "Leap, Don't Sleep" file, knowing that all I have to do is fifteen seconds of work to fulfill my agreement with myself. This often has turned into as many as three hours of writing and research.

Urgent vs. Important. The 80/20 Rule

The Italian economist Pareto tells us from studies that 80 percent of our accomplishments come from 20 percent of our activities, that is to say that only 20 percent of our time really accomplishes very much or is really productive. And if we're honest with ourselves, we know that's true. Sometimes it might be as little as 10 percent. I've been there. If you were to pause at the end of an average day and re-run the day's activities in your mind, chances are you'd feel somewhat guilty or disappointed with the difference between what you intended to do and what you actually accomplished. Did you ever say to yourself at the end of a tiring day, "I've done absolutely nothing all day." On the one hand you're right, in that you have done little to advance your own goals or agenda, whereas you've probably done more for other people than you wanted to or needed to. In other words it wasn't important to you.

We end up having to spend too much time on *urgent* matters if we don't spend enough time on *important* matters. For instance, one client was spending 75 percent of her time solving employee problems — such as inter-department conflict, absenteeism, and performance issues — while insufficient time was spent at the hiring stage with interviewing, orientation, and training. Her *urgent* activities resulted from her failure to invest more adequate time on the *important* activities. The dilemma here, of course, is that if we don't do what needs to be done in the beginning, then the ill effects of our omission multiply, and our energies are refocused so that we're in a "putting out fires" mode.

If we put off doing what is important, it will likely turn into what's urgent. Is that good or bad? Well, for some people, the last-minute rush is what gets them going and stimulated, especially some journalists who have a story deadline. For the rest of us, that's not the case. This is an area where *getting control* and *taking charge* is what it's all about. Most of us have a huge master list, some of us have it organized on one sheet or on the computer, while others among us have sticky notes all over the refrigerator, the computer and any mirror that will hold them. After a while these become part of the landscape, and they no longer stand out as important tasks to be done.

The first thing to do is to get all these jobs or tasks which have to be done onto one sheet or file. Put everything you do on this list, whether it be business, job, or personal. Now you have everything in one place. Now you can decide what to work on today.

Every evening before you close out the day, take five minutes or so to look over your list, cross off what you've completed. (Actually it's good to do this immediately after you complete a project as it gives you a visual sense of achievement, thereby fueling you with energy to go forward.) Then select five or six important items from this master list for tomorrow. Write or print them onto a separate list. Have a good idea how long they might take because it's a bad idea to overload yourself with unrealistic time-laden tasks. Add 50 percent to your original estimate for each project, especially for tasks like writing a report or working on a budget.

The next step is critical and powerful. Decide which of these five or six items you will start on first tomorrow. Pick the most difficult, the one you keep putting off or the one that will have the biggest impact on your goals. Having selected this item, clear your desk and put material related to this project on there so that this is the first thing you see in the morning.

Why is this powerful?

Because by selecting and focusing, even for a minute, on this difficult item, your inner computer, your subconscious, will go to work for you overnight to get your "system" in rhythm for a productive outcome tomorrow. When you do this, you have taken charge of your day, rather than looking over the master list when you arrive at the desk and being overwhelmed by the quantity of outstanding work you have to do.

In this way you'll be less likely to get buried in the *urgent zone*, having taken the time to visit the *important zone* where you did some planning that will now pay off.

Learn how to say "NO!"

It's very hard to be in charge of your own life and your own destiny if you just can't say NO! every once in a while. When we can't say NO!, we allow other people to run our lives or to have a greater influence on what we do than we ourselves have. Part of this weakness is the need to be liked or to fit in — as in a fraternity, a club, or a committee.

I know one lady who is forever running from one charity to another, chairing at least one committee, and keeping house for her husband and two teenagers at the same time. She's constantly on the phone and often gives the appearance of being burnt out. Why? Because she just can't say NO! Many people in this group are caring and contributing people, often more selfless than is good for them, and usually afraid of offending or alienating others.

Of course the real problem is simply that they don't know how to say NO! in a way that will not make them

feel bad. Here's *how* to say NO! if you fit into that category. Just practice this two-step formula until it becomes
an automatic response:

   1. Apologize (immediately) that you can't help
       them. Be firm and not wimpy, and give a reason,
       for example: "Bob, I'm sorry, I just can't sit on
       any more committees this year. I've got a full
       load and I just can't take on any more. I really
       wish I could help." Of course they will press
       you, reminding you that you're indispensable
       and that the whole thing will collapse if you're
       not there to monitor it. Don't weaken, think of
       YOU — they're not!

   2. Offer an alternative suggestion: "You might ask
       Barbara. She's just finished that X project and I
       think she would be great for your program; also
       she might enjoy this opportunity." They've
       probably already asked her and she turned them
       down, so they'll plead with you. Don't falter,
       say, "No, I'm sorry, I really am." and leave it
       there.

This will become easier with practice. And instead of
feeling guilty, give yourself a pat on the back: you've just
conquered what might be your biggest cause of overload
and stress. Now you can just say NO! And, as you get
more practiced at saying NO!, you'll be better prepared to
respond to situations in the future.

RECAP

1. Read the *The 15-Second Principle* by Al Secunda.
2. Understand the difference between *Urgent* and *Important*.
3. Learn how to say NO!

Application Exercise

Write down:

1. One or two goals that you're having difficulty accomplishing.
2. What is preventing you from making progress? procrastination _____ no plan _____ unclear goals _____ other _____
3. Here's what I'm going to do, starting tomorrow:

   a) _____

   b) _____
4. DO IT NOW!

D

DELEGATE AND EMPOWER YOUR PEOPLE

*No matter how brilliant you are or how techni-
cally capable, it's tough to be effective as a
leader unless you get the willing cooperation
of others.*

— PETER DRUCKER

The effective manager, owner, or supervisor is that person who has mastered the art of delegation and empowerment with his or her employees. Delegation is not to be confused with dumping work on other people with a disregard for overloading them, leading to *de-motivation*. True delegation means giving responsibility to others with the resources and the training to do the job. Many of us are poor delegators, and as a result we miss out on the benefits that result from mastering this skill.

How can we do a better job of delegating?
1. Share information.
2. Untie their hands.
3. Have faith in their potential.
4. Back them up.

Share information

When it comes to delegating effectively, we cannot win unless we give the person the information to do the job. Now this sounds rather simplistic — and you might say, "Well that's easy, I already give them information. I tell them what has to be done. They just have to go and do it." The problem is that often we just don't give sufficient information to the people to do the job we're delegating to them. It might be something simple such as a hotel manager who went out of town for a day, forgetting to give the combination of the safe to the person she put in charge. Or a shipping manager in a client's distribution company who took a day off to attend his son's graduation, but did not inform his employees that one of their co-workers was in charge, putting the delegatee in an awkward spot when she had to make a couple of tough decisions.

Untie their hands

Often the information that's not given is what is most needed. For instance, what does the person do if a certain problem occurs? What level of flexibility are you giving? I was conducting a seminar for about a hundred people in Springfield, Missouri. At lunchtime I went along with some of the attendees to the restaurant where a buffet was laid out for diners. I said to the host who appeared to be in charge that I would just take a plate of food from the buffet, pay for it and take it to eat back in the conference room so I could relax my voice and keep an eye on items that the attendees had left in the room. The host said, "You can't take the buffet out of the restaurant." I asked why not. She said, "It's policy." After explaining to her that I was conducting a seminar for most of the people now in her dining room, and that if anything I should be offered a complimentary meal — let alone being barred from the taking my meal to another location — she reluctantly acquiesced and allowed me to take the meal out of the restaurant.

This is a classic example of where we assign responsibility to another, and then we tie their hands by not allowing them to make decisions based on their good judgment in the situation. We can all learn a lesson from the famous Nordstrom's policy where it says, "Rule # 1: Use your good judgment in all situations. There will be no additional rules."

I recommend you have a checklist for occasions when you're going to delegate to someone, especially for the first time. Apart from the more obvious tasks that have to be accomplished, list some things that could happen that require decision-making by this person. Show them how they should be handled, and what flexibility they have in applying the rules. Remember the Customer Service Recovery Program and our mission to be more proactive.

It's hard to talk about delegation without talking about *empowerment*. What does empowerment mean? It means giving people the freedom to use the power they already have to make decisions. Some time ago, I was hired to put on a series of seminars at a military base for the support services: food and beverage department, gift shops, recreation, and security services. When I interviewed the co-coordinator this program, she asked me not to mention *empowerment* in my presentation. When I asked why not, she told me they'd had a motivational speaker the previous year who was very good, but that nothing changed. In other words, they were no more empowered than they were before the speaker came.

Upon further questioning I discovered that several people at the head of these departments did not attend the training. Either they felt that they knew it all, or that they would not feel comfortable sitting at a seminar along with their own people, their co-workers. I had the impression that the speakers were just brought in to "motivate" the employees so they'd all be pumped up and do a better job for another year.

Unfortunately it's not that simple. In today's very competitive world, your success as a manager is measured by the performance of your people. More than ever, you depend on the willing and active participation of your employees to achieve your company goals. You can no longer expect unconditional loyalty and commitment from them, so your ability to delegate successfully is related to your success at motivating your employees.

Ken Blanchard and John Carlos wrote one of those short easy-to-read books called *Empowerment Takes*

More Than a Minute, a down-to-earth lesson on true empowerment. They emphasize that the first rule is to share information with everyone. You might think this isn't wise or necessary. Wrong. The fact is that in today's fast-paced, competitive world, with everything happening instantly, there's just no way that you can be miserly in extending training and growth to only a select few of your employees. If you look hard, you'll find that almost every person you have working for you is capable of achieving much more than is apparent on the surface. Also the fact is that today you need far more involvement by your employees in the running of the business. They have invaluable input about the problems that dog your business. They are the people who have many of the answers if we are just smart enough to come down off our high horse and ask them. Zig Ziglar, the great motivator and author, reminds us of the four most important words to say to your employees, "What is your opinion?"

But, they need information to act upon and to perform a better job. They need to understand what's going on in the business: are you making money, losing money, having too few customers return? Are you on budget, way off, or pretty close? They need to know why certain decisions are made, which on the surface make no sense to them. In short, they need and want to know how the business is run, and how they fit in.

Have faith in their potential

Part of the reason for hesitation to delegate is our fear that the people we're delegating to may fail. Or, we may procrastinate because we don't have the time to teach them what they need to know in order to take on this responsibility.

Dealing with fear of failure is handled by taking the time to cover all bases of authority, expectations, and responsibility. (Of course you can't just delegate to someone who does not have the skill, talent, and ability to do the job.)

You should delegate not only the menial jobs, but also the more significant ones. Employees will see this as a vote of confidence. How many times have you been pleasantly surprised by how an employee shone in a new role, or when given more responsibility? If we recognize and feed the potential of our people, we will become masters of delegation.

Back them up

To back up your employees means that you allow them to take some risks. You allow them to be flexible and creative, while all the time they are trying to do their best in using good judgment. Do you think that host in the restaurant felt secure that she would be backed up by her boss if I was spotted carrying the buffet plate out of the restaurant, that she would be penalized, maybe fired for breaking an inflexible rule? This doesn't mean that you're going to agree with everything the employee does in your absence. What it does mean is that you support the decisions she makes, and that when necessary you will coach her on improvements or changes in approach that might be made on future occasions to better handle the situation.

It's important that an employee is acknowledged for making a decision when one needs to be made, however difficult or misguided it might have been. Risk taking is part of growing and developing, and as long as this is done in a responsible way with the customer's or company's best interests in mind, you have an invaluable employee who may be destined for great things, and who will certainly contribute in a big way to your being more successful through his or her efforts and dedication.

RECAP
1. Share information.
2. Untie their hands.
3. Have faith in their potential.
4. Back them up.

Application Exercise

Write down:
1. What are some items of information you will start sharing with your employees tomorrow?
2. What is preventing you from doing this now?
3. What will you do, and when, to remove these obstacles?
4. DO IT NOW!

O

OPERATE LIKE AN OWNER

Owners focus on results regardless of who's watching.

— UNKNOWN

This is an important statement because today the world is such that if we only see ourselves as working for someone else, we're way behind in our thinking. And that is how we'll remain. What I'm saying is that we are responsible for our own lives, our families, our performance at work, the amount of money we save, how much we spend or lose. If at work we believe that all problems we cause will be magically taken care of, or hidden, we're kidding ourselves.

But, for many, that is what a job life was like in the "good old days." We were "carried" by the more productive and responsible workers in the department or the business. We came to work and left after eight hours. We kept our noses clean, didn't make any waves, and we were rewarded twice a month with a paycheck, and maybe a turkey at Christmas.

This life is gone. Today, you must be able to show what you've produced. Of course, on the factory floor, this is obvious in the materials or products coming off the line; but what about you, Mr. Salesman or Ms. Supervisor, or Mr. Accountant? What have you done today that has impacted the growth or profitability of the company, or of yourself?

How do you operate like an owner?
1. Imagine it's your own business.
2. Write down your goals.
3. Discipline yourself

Imagine it's your own business

So, what would you do differently if it were your own business? Did you ever observe a tradesperson — plumber, roofer, window cleaner — at work in your house or apartment? Do you remember thinking what a mess they left behind after finishing the job? Maybe they didn't clean up adequately, or they were inconsiderate of your time by coming late, or by not turning up at all so you had to call. Were they employees or the owners of the business? If they were the owners, you should re-think before hiring them again. If they were employees, have you called the owners to discuss the performance?

The chances are that if the reputable owner of the company came to conduct repairs or renovations, he or she would be more likely to do a great job, and leave your place in a clean condition. And why? So that you'll call him or her again when the need arises, or so you'll help the business grow by referring it to friends and associates.

People who eventually become owners of businesses, big or small, pretty much seem to have operated as if they owned the business wherever they worked. There are, also, many successful people out there who have no desire to own the business, but who operate as if they do.

You can tell pretty quickly who the "owners" are in most companies. They're not always the people with the bubbliest personalities or the best dressed and groomed, although some have those attributes. In fact they are recognized by their general attitude of responsibility, their desire to grow and expand their horizons, and their interest in the future success of the company. They are ethical, generally respectful, and trustworthy. They also are entrepreneurial, often risk takers and innovators.

Some well-known companies — such as 3M, Hewlett Packard, Southwest Airlines, Motorola, and Microsoft, encourage ownership thinking by making it the norm, often requiring individuals to be initiators and executors of new ideas without waiting for direction. Of course they give their employees the freedom and the resources to experiment and to be creative. Tom Peters, in his book, *Brand You*, tells us to look hard at what contribution we make to our organization. He says to write down what two to four skills or accomplishments you are known for in your company today; what one or two more achievements you are planning to be known for next year; how is the current project you're working on challenging you; and what new information or skills have you learned in the last 90 days? All this kind of activity will help you think and act more like an owner.

Write down your goals

Only about 5 percent of adults have written goals. I went for years without them, and if I were pompous I would probably say I did well despite them. The fact is, however, that I didn't ever feel that I was accomplishing very much before I started writing down my goals. You see, it's very difficult to focus on achieving anything substantial if you haven't written it down. There are so many distractions and so much going on simultaneously that unless there is point of focus — your written goals with deadlines — you won't make much real progress.

Many people don't write their goals simply because they don't know what their goals are, or they are only vaguely aware of what they want to achieve or what they want to be. I spoke to a class of high school teenagers in a low-income neighborhood school. When I asked who had any goals, only two hands went up. Come to think of it, when I was their age, I wasn't too sure of what I wanted to do either. Furthermore I didn't know how to go about setting goals even if anyone bothered to tell me I should have some.

As you read this, you may be already well into your career and adult life, so I don't want to address you as if you're still in school — although I suppose we're all in the school of life. What I told those teenagers can apply to you or me, and that is that our goals often come from our interests and from our talents.

In order to stimulate discussion, I asked the young people to tell me individually what they were good at, or in what areas they thought they might be talented. From that discussion they began to connect possible goals with their talents or interests.

Most of them were in a program where they had to work as well as attend school, and they were graded on their attendance and performance at their part-time jobs. None of them liked their jobs, mostly fast food, and when asked why, they blamed customers, co-workers, and managers for their "unhappiness." Does that sound familiar? Can you see in your mind a time, or even a lot of times, when you have been in that frame of mind?

We all have at some time, but when it's the norm, it's time to do something. It's time to get out of what you're doing or develop a connection between the job and what turns you on. We may have limited options when we're teenagers about what part-time job we take to make and save some money, but if we're going to whine about it because it doesn't have a "cool" label to it, or because it's hard or boring, then we'll likely never rise above *average* in any job.

It comes back to having some kind of goal. Why am I doing this? Why not something else? What do I get out of this? One young man in the class enjoyed babysitting, so he felt one day he might manage and eventually own a childcare center, which is good. But then I asked him about the fast-food job, why he didn't like it — he wasn't really sure.

The dilemma for him might be the same for an adult who is well into her third or fourth job, or still in her first career. Why am I doing this? I'm not happy.

Contrast this with someone you know who is obviously enjoying what she or he does, someone who seems to really care about the job and about the company. What's different about them, you ask?

It gets back to having a connection. Could it be that in my job I make a difference in the lives of others, and would that be good? Do I believe that this job is preparing me for greater things to come by the experience and discipline that I am exposed to? Is my contribution to this job such that lots of people depend on me; therefore I *count* in the scheme of things? Is there something I've overlooked in this job that would make it more interesting?

I presented a half-day seminar to a hotel employee group on customer service. Rather than preaching about the importance of giving excellent service to every guest who came in the door, I had the employees discuss what could be fun about making all their guests feel welcome, important, and comfortable. In other words I helped them to figure out "what's in it for me?," besides the pay or the tips. After the seminar, one young lady came up to me and said that she had planned to quit in two days, but that now she had a better understanding of the possibilities of the job, and she was going to stay and take a different approach and a different attitude to hotel guests and her co-workers. She was going to have a goal and think like an owner.

Whatever connection you can come up with becomes the foundation to your goal or your revised goal.

Discipline yourself

For many the word discipline seems rather alien — even harsh, like punishment, control, or excess regulation. You don't like the sound of it — and, as a result you don't practice it. But, without discipline there is no great success.

With discipline, you have mastery over your very existence, power over your own domain. Discipline requires conscious effort and some guts. Zig Ziglar says, "When you're tough on yourself, life is infinitely easier on you."

Discipline means taking charge of your life, doing things that you're inclined to not want to do, such as stepping outside of the box of habit. For some, it might be getting up an hour earlier to get a head start on a project; for another, it might be going to the health club to work-out on a cold wet day when you'd much rather stay inside; and for yet another, it might be getting on the computer to respond to emails instead of watching TV.

Know yourself

It helps a lot if you have gotten to know and acknowledge your weaknesses, the factors that prevent you from moving to the next level. For me, discipline means being more focused, focused on what has to be done today, my priorities. I tend to get distracted easily. I'm all over the place, juggling many tasks at once, often not finishing any single one in a timely manner, like my procrastination in writing this book, which I talked about in an earlier chapter. As I've worked on this book, I've become more aware of what causes me to be distracted, and I have taken tough action to resist it. As a result I am making better progress through being more focused.

Why was I so far behind? Probably because I didn't set myself any goals of completion. Why? Probably because I didn't think it was important enough. Why? Probably because I had no advance excitement about the outcome of having my book in print. Why? Probably because I didn't think about it as one of the most important goals in my life. (As I write this now, I'm being a bit introspective and coaching myself into better discipline. "Just do it" is a good coaching call for self-discipline.)

I have read many times that you have to have passion about what you're doing in order to do it well. I didn't seem to have enough passion about writing this book. I asked myself, should I even be writing this? Who am I to think that I'm a writer? I read about Steven King, the best-selling author who, early on when he was first writing, worked a couple of jobs during the day, and then typed his manuscripts right into the early hours of the morning, as he tried to support his family. And I thought, he's just naturally a brilliant writer, hugely creative, incredibly inspired, motivated by great passion — and hunger. Maybe I'm not hungry enough, maybe I don't have the talent to write. Excuses. All excuses! Excuses breed a lack of discipline.

My big push to be more disciplined came after I started telling people at my seminars that I was writing a book. I told clients, friends, acquaintances; and I printed that fact in my bio-introduction, which was read out whenever I spoke at a convention. At first I thought, this will give me some credibility add a little punch for meeting planners and booking agents. What it did do was to cause some of these people to ask me later how the book was coming along. Well, you can imagine how that forced me to get back on track, get focused, and become more disciplined. It reminded me how I finally quit smoking over twelve years ago. I told people that I had quit smoking from the first day. When I had tried to quit previously, I used to tell people that I was *trying* to quit; then I'd accept a cigarette — just one, which of course put me back on them for another year.

Discipline has made me get this far despite the frequent distractions and the feelings that I should be doing something else while I'm waiting for inspiration.

The power of intention

Discipline comes when you have true intention. Some call it commitment. If you invite someone to a party and he says he'll try to get there, chances are he has little, if any, intention of going. There's a young man who did some repair work and painting at my house. I learned fairly quickly that when he said he'd "try and come back at noon" on Thursday, I'd be lucky if I saw him by one o' clock — or even on that day at all. Thankfully, most people are more reliable than that, but I sensed that this person was not at all disciplined — though a fine craftsman. I also determined that he should be making a lot more money as he was so talented. But he was not disciplined, so you got what you paid for — delayed job completion, poor follow-up to correct problems, and too many social distractions. I could see some of the same in myself.

You should be aware of what you're good at as well. How can you capitalize on your talents, on those things that come easy to you, on the best time of day to do a particular task? Be more aware of how you function, and when you function best. For me it's the morning. Although I'm not a very early riser like many entrepreneurs and successful people, once I'm up and about, I can be very productive if I'll only avoid morning distractions like getting glued to the news on television, or having my attention diverted while searching for something in a file or a book, or reading through my mail when it could wait till later.

Discipline comes with practice and sometimes a lot of self-denial. The great athletes became great through the discipline of practice and resisting the temptation to take it easy and bask in the comforts of life that beckon us at every moment. The great entrepreneurs and leaders have a passion and focus that pushes them to do what unsuccessful people don't like to do.

RECAP
1. Imagine it's your own business.
2. Write down your goals.
3. Discipline yourself.

Application Exercise

Write down:
1. What are some things you would do differently if you owned the business you work for?
2. What are your written goals, and are they visible?
3. What specific areas or projects have you given up on that you could revive?
4. What will you start on as a result of studying this material?
5. DO IT NOW!

<u>N</u>

NEVER STOP TRYING

Persistent people find success when others end in failure.

— UNKNOWN

O bviously if you are to follow this advice of *never stop trying*, you'll need some serious discipline as we talked about in the last chapter. You'll also need to be firmly focused on what you want to accomplish. It's about perseverance. It's about how you deal with change. Quotations abound to inspire us in this endeavor: "Great works are performed not by strength, but by perseverance" (Samuel Johnson); "With ordinary talent and extraordinary perseverance, all things are attainable" (Sir Thomas Foxwell Buxton). "Persistent people find success when others end in failure" (Unknown).

How can we motivate ourselves to keep trying?
1. Learn from the success of others.
2. Get out of your own way.
3. Learn from your failures

Learn from the success of others

A great example of perseverance is the following biography chart:

At age 22 ....he failed his first business venture
At age 23..........he was defeated for the Legislature
At age 24..............he had failed in another business
At age 25 ....he was finally elected to Legislature
At age 27 ....he had a nervous breakdown
At age 29.....................he was defeated for Speaker
At age 31 ....he was defeated for Elector
At age 34...................he was defeated for Congress
At age 37..........................he got elected to Congress
At age 39.....................he lost his Congressional seat
At age 46 ....he was defeated for Senate
At age 47...........................he lost for Vice President
At age 49 ....he was defeated for Senate
At age 51...........................he was elected President

HE WAS ABRAHAM LINCOLN!

One of my greatest sources of research and inspiration is the television program, "Biography." Whenever I'm at home in the evening, this is my favorite show. Obviously it is about famous and infamous people, and most of them would be considered to be very successful. I noticed a pattern amongst these heroes, which I constantly try to emulate, and that is to stay focused and be dogged about what I feel passionate about, in order to make it come to fruition. We've read it about those no longer here, such as Albert Einstein, Benjamin Franklin, Thomas Edison, and Mother Teresa. We've experienced it in our lifetime with Bill Gates, Lee Iacocca, Walt Disney, and Colonel Sanders. All of them, in common, had great setbacks and adversities, but they kept going.

Colonel Sanders was turned down over one thousand times before someone said yes to his chicken recipe. Walt Disney was turned down three hundred and two times before he got financial aid for his dream of creating the happiest place on earth. These are examples of people who became great successes because they didn't give up; they never stopped trying.

Get out of your own way

How do you get in your own way? You do so by blocking your own success in some way: either by giving up, by making excuses for inaction, or by not focusing on your goals.

Why do we so often give up? One reason is that we're afraid of failing and of being perceived as a failure. We've all been there. When I was invited to become a management consultant with a reputable firm in the United States (while still living in London), I was terrified of failing, and what others at home might think, especially after the great farewell party they threw for me at my previous job. Early in the new job I struggled with the new environment, while supervising people who knew much more about the work than I did. I felt somewhat inadequate and

I found it hard to give clear directions. I was feeling a bit sorry for myself, using the excuse that I had never done this work before, and that I also had to deal with the language barrier. "England and America are divided by a common language," said George Bernard Shaw. These were all *excuses*, not *reasons* that prevented me from succeeding in the beginning. <u>The reason I wasn't successful was buried in the excuses I was making.</u> There was no logical basis for those excuses other than plain old fear. Then I remembered some of the apprehensions I'd had in previous jobs and experiences and how I had come through by persevering.

Learn from your failures

Failure is the great educator, the great opener of the doors of success. If you were to sit down with a pen and randomly write down all the failures you can remember in your life, chances are you learned something from each, whether you're prepared to admit it or not.

If you're not experiencing failure frequently in your job and in your life, you are probably not accomplishing great things. Those people we mentioned earlier who never gave up experienced many failures — probably many more than you or I put together.

What did they learn? Well, first they learned many ways that one of their ideas didn't work. They learned why it didn't work that way. As a result of trial and error they learned new approaches to solving problems. They also learned that they never would have accomplished their success if they hadn't learned from failure and kept trying. There's not much value in learning from your failures if you then become *inactive* in order to avoid any future flops.

Barbara De Angelis, in her book, *Confidence — Finding it and Living It*, says, "To succeed, you have to do something and be very bad at it for a while." I was so glad the first time I read that was during my early days of speaking professionally. I was with one of those seminar companies that sent contract speakers like me all over the world presenting one-day seminars — four or five in one week.

My very first seminar was probably my worst presentation, and then I had some more that were best forgotten. All the speakers were judged by their evaluations ratings, which were sent in to the seminar company's headquarters immediately after each seminar.

My ratings were very poor at first, especially on some of the topics that I was not yet comfortable presenting. As a result the company cut back on my assignments, which meant that I made less money from speaking and from the sales commissions.

I considered going back to the business I knew, and where I made much more money — running multiple hotels. It was very tempting, and the only thing that stopped me was the fact that I desperately wanted to speak and to share practical ideas with many people, and I wanted to be good at it. Luckily I had saved my money well during the good times, so I could afford to go through the learning phase for a little while longer.

I can now say that I have learned more in the last six years than I had in the previous twenty. Could it be that I've had more failures? Absolutely! And had I just given up instead of learning from those failures, I wouldn't be at the point I am right now — which took a lot longer than I expected; but it was more than worth the effort and the disappointments along the way.

RECAP

1. Learn from the success of others.
2. Get out of your own way.
3. Learn from your failures

Application Exercise

Write down:

1. What are the names of your heroes in business, sports, the arts, or other areas?
2. What obstacles have you overcome in your life, despite the odds and your feelings of inadequacy at the time?
3. What recent job or personal failures have you learned lessons from, and what results have come from those lessons — or what results do you expect to come in the future?
4. DO IT NOW!

8

T
TEACH OTHERS
WHAT YOU
KNOW

*Empowerment comes from teaching others
things they can do to become less dependent
on you.*

— KEN BLANCHARD

When you plan to teach what you learn to others, you immediately become a better student, a better teacher, and a better leader. You'll also gain more time to be creative and to extend your own knowledge and experience. If you fail to do this, you'll be doing everything yourself, you'll have no succession plan, and your effectiveness as a leader will be weak.

How can you teach others what you know?
1. Immediately share what you've learned.
2. Make it interesting and applicable.
3. Make a list of tips, suggestions, or information you can share with others.

Immediately share what you've learned

When you return to your office from a convention or important meeting, you should have a plan to disseminate all information that other people need or could benefit by as soon as possible. This rarely happens, because of poor planning. By the time you return from an event, your desk and computer have already been loaded with stuff that needs your attention, so the importance of the material you've just acquired has diminished in favor of those "urgent" items now taunting you.

I find that if I physically do what needs to be done while I'm still on the road, or in the hotel room before I leave, this puts me way ahead of the curve. It might be that I need to do a short memo, or a summary of the highlights of the meeting or seminar. How much easier it is to accomplish that while you are in the uninterrupted environment of the hotel room, or even waiting at the airport.

When I ran a group of hotels, my managers often attended conventions and seminars. I encouraged them, after each event, to make a summary of what they learned and present it to their staff in a training environment, with a copy of the highlights to me so I could monitor results. Another benefit was that I was able to measure the return on investment related to the expense of multiple attendances at these events. At first there was some resistance, but everyone soon realized the benefits, both to them and to their employees.

Make it interesting and applicable

All information shared must have a purpose, not only for the communicator of the information, but also for the receiver. Often we teach some of our great knowledge to others, only to find little or very mild interest. Old war stories told to a grandson who has no concept of what you went through, nor any interest in the topic will not gain much attentiveness.

I presented a seminar on interpersonal skills to a group in a manufacturing plant. One lady said on her evaluation that the information really helped her to identify the causes of conflict between her and her teenage daughter, while she had no problems getting along with her coworkers. In other words, the information was applicable to her in one way, while it was applicable in other ways to someone else. You have to be sure that the information has meaning and some benefit for the recipient. There must be a link, a connection, between what you share and what the recipient needs and/or wants.

Make a list of tips, suggestions, or information you can share with others

Take a half hour to yourself and write down some tasks or techniques that you could teach your staff, your colleagues, or your family members that would enhance their competence on the job or in completing a particular task. We often see people tackling a job or a problem, and we just know that there's a better and simpler way of doing it. We know how we would do it. But because we think we're too busy to show them, or that it will take too long, we let it go and thus prevent their possible success — and ultimately our own.

RECAP

1. Immediately share what you've learned.
2. Make it interesting and applicable.
3. Make a list of tips, suggestions, or information you can share with others.

Application Exercise

Write down:

1. What are some shortfalls you are aware of in others — coworkers, subordinates, family members, or friends — that might be overcome by your sharing of information or techniques with them.

2. How will you present this information in a way that is respectful, and in a way that you are connecting with the other person's needs or wants?

3. When will you begin to help a specific person by sharing your knowledge and skills — today, tomorrow, next Monday?

4. DO IT NOW!

S
SOLVE PROBLEMS TODAY!

All problems become smaller if you don't
dodge them, but confront them.

— WILLIAM F. HALSEY

D o you ever get the feeling that we are put on earth to solve problems? Where would our minds be if we weren't solving problems on a daily basis? Probably dead — at least dead bored. At my seminars I often ask the question, "How many people here would say you spend a lot of time solving problems?" Practically all hands are raised. And yet there are many problems that go unsolved — just like some crimes. When I ask for a show of hands from people who have no problems, I see no hands. That alone must tell you that life is a problem-solving process.

We are told that when you're selling a product or service to a customer, you should be showing that customer how to solve problems; in that way her perception of value will cause her to buy. But we also get many false promises of how a problem will be solved — reminding us to be cautious and wary of the snake-oil sellers.

When I worked in the corporate world before starting my own business, companies used the phrase "problem solving skills" in the recruiting advertising. A good resume told the potential hirer what a great problem solver you are — with examples in your former job listed under "accomplishments." If you're not solving problems, then you're probably not making great strides on your career ladder.

How can you master the art of problem solving?
1. Define the problem.
2. List the causes of the problem.
3. Write down all possible solutions.
4. Select the best possible solution.
5. Implement your plan.
6. Follow-up and evaluate progress.

Define the problem

I believe that many of our problems go unsolved because we fail to identify or define them. You ask a friend, a colleague, or a spouse, "What's the problem?" How do they answer? Usually by saying "Nothing." And the more you press them to explain their behavior, the less progress you make. Charles Kettering, the inventor and developer of the first electrical ignition system for automobiles, said, "A problem well stated is half solved."

I remember one day my assistant seemed a little down and was not her usual cheerful and enthusiastic self. I asked her if anything was wrong. She gave me an unconvincing "No." Later I managed to drag out of her that she was upset over something I said to her a couple of days before in frustration. She, unknown to me, had taken it personally, believing that I was indirectly accusing her of being stupid. She had been stewing over it ever since, whereas I had forgotten the episode and I was otherwise preoccupied.

As we talked about how I had unwittingly offended her, I realized an apology was appropriate, and that I needed to be more considerate and respectful next time. This type of problem is not uncommon and it can lead to other problems, such as lost productivity, poor communications, and so on.

A constant problem for some clients is employee turnover. If you're worried about employee turnover, you must clearly define the problem. Rather than continuing to say, "Our turnover is terrible," you might want to quantify it in relation to the industry norm, or in relation to your budget or standards. "We had a 55 percent turnover rate last year, 20 points above what we consider acceptable in our industry."

List the causes of the problem

It's hard to solve any problem unless you can identify its cause. If you go to a doctor with a problem, he'll likely ask what caused the injury or symptoms if it's not readily obvious. The causes may vary. For instance, if you're getting repeated headaches, you may need glasses — or perhaps you're not eating regularly, or your job is very stressful.

If turnover is a problem in your company, what are some of the causes? Are people leaving for better pay?

Have terminations increased due to incompetence or misbehavior? Is there a weakness in your supervision? Are working conditions questionable? Is equipment out of date?

Write down all possible solutions

This is easier than you might think if you consider that solutions to problems must have some association with the causes. As a famous person said, "Every problem contains the seeds of its own solution." Take the turnover problem, for example. If one of the causes is termination through incompetence, then a possible solution would be to conduct better training and follow-up. If many people are leaving because of low pay, a possible solution is to review your pay structure and see how competitive you are in your industry.

Select the best possible solution(s)

From all the possible solutions, select one that will have the most impact, and of course one that your budget will allow. If a possible solution to a problem — such as a photo copier that has constant break-downs — is to buy a new one, you may not have the ready funds to do so, but you might get by with a loaner until some major repairs are carried out.

In the case of your turnover problem, it may not be possible to raise everyone's pay at once to compete in the marketplace, but you certainly can institute an incentive program to reward employees for improved sales, productivity, and profits, all of which pay for your extra outlay.

You may select more than one specific solution or action, depending on the problem and available resources.

For instance you may, in the case of high turnover, send your manager to a workshop on retaining and motivating employees.

Implement your plan

For many this is the toughest part of problem solving — mainly because it requires you to do something that you're not used to doing. Many companies have spent thousands of dollars on consultants who analyzed and made recommendations for operating problems they (the companies) had, but they never implemented the solutions they agreed upon. They buried themselves in inaction. (I know all about that, as I've done it many times myself.) The great benefit to me while writing this book is that I know I had better be practicing what I preach; and that is where some of my motivation comes from — as well as being constantly focused on my goal of holding a published book in my hand as I autograph it for a buyer.

Implementation must come with a plan where everyone involved is committed to success. Even those in disagreement must be persuaded to give it an honest try. That's where *your* powers of persuasion come in. You have to be a good communicator to explain and coach others into this corrective action.

Follow-up and evaluate progress

Whenever something new happens — a new project, a new menu item in a restaurant, a new work schedule, or a new process on a production line — it is rare that all goes perfectly. There are kinks to be ironed out, employees to reassure, adjustments to be made. If you just implement and go directly on vacation without the all-important follow-up, you're committing suicide.

But what great satisfaction there is in a changed status quo, a problem that is solved, or a tough project that finishes on time. How great the motivation to move on to other challenges when you have conquered this singular problem. These are great reasons to make follow-up an important and invaluable part of the process.

RECAP

1. Define the Problem.
2. List the causes of the problem.
3. Write down all possible solutions.
4. Select the best possible solution.
5. Implement your plan.
6. Follow-up and evaluate progress.

Application Exercise

Write down:
1. Identify one or more problems you have right now, business or personal.
2. Use the six-step formula for each problem
3. Write down a date when you will implement it.
4. DO IT NOW!

L

LAUGH, AND
ENJOY HUMOR

*Among those whom I admire I can find no
common denominator, but among those whom I
love, I can: all of them make me laugh.*

— W.H. AUDEN

Humor is our salvation, our comfort, our stress
reliever, and our source of creativity. Ever since
my early days in the orphanage in Ireland, I have
a firm belief in the power of humor in all of life's challenges. I have proof that it works, not just for me, but for
others whom I've seen first-hand. Doctors, psychologists,
humorists, and even anthropologists, have written much
about its great benefits.

Why should we use humor? What are the benefits?
1. Humor aids learning and memory.
2. Humor builds rapport.
3. Humor reduces tension and stress.
4. Humor heals illness.
5. Humor stimulates creativity.

Humor aids learning and memory

You probably remember that learning was the most fun when you were in kindergarten. You laughed a lot. You had all kinds of colors as you sketched and used crayons. Your teachers were fun. Even at the orphanage, I remember it being relatively pleasant at that young age. The songs, poems and experiences from that time stayed with us, and when we think about those experiences, we can't help but smile with happy nostalgia.

Sadly, we seemed to grow out of that kind of learning as we got older and went to high school. Teaching became serious. We were admonished for laughing in class. We got bored, and some of us took any opportunity to skip class.

The great teachers of today are those who are trying to revive humor and fun in teaching because they know that learning can be fun, and retention of the material is more likely if students are enjoying the learning process. I have a chance to visit with students in my occasional talks at high schools, and the feedback I've gotten from them is that they learn better and are more enthusiastic about their studies with teachers who incorporate fun and interaction into the lessons classes, regardless of the topic.

We can see the benefits of humor in advertising. Remember that great punch line for a Wendy's burger,

"Where's the Beef?", and remember the wacky duck in the commercial for Aflac Insurance. Unlike other commercials that we saw daily, these stood out in a big way. And they had a huge impact on their respective businesses because they were memorable and fun — two characteristics that inevitably go well together.

Many years ago John Cleese, the co-writer and producer of Monty Python, founded a training company in England. The company has since merged with an American company called Coastal. This company, with the active involvement of Cleese and other comedy actors, has produced dozens of training videos with great humor content to make many important points in management and customer service topics.

Humor builds rapport

Victor Borge, the great Danish entertainer, said, "Humor is the shortest distance between two people." If you can make someone laugh or smile, you can generate business, you can build rapport, and you can reduce conflict and intimidation.

Former President Ronald Reagan was known as the "Great Communicator." Part of his charisma came from his ability to use humor to make others feel at ease under difficult circumstances. In 1981 when he was shot, he was lying on the stretcher, his wife Nancy looking down at him with tears in her eyes, worried he wasn't going to make it. He smiled as he reached out and held her hand and said, "Honey, I forgot to duck." A year after his presidency, I saw him speak at a convention in Orlando. Five minutes after he started speaking there was a loud bang outside the auditorium. The room went silent as Mr. Reagan paused. He looked in the direction from where the sound had come, then he looked back at the audience and said, "I think they missed me that time." The audience loved him.

Humor reduces tension and stress

Today, tension and stress abound in our lives: the pressure of deadlines, the urgency of the telephone and the e-mails that need responses, and the juggling of many projects and responsibilities. We all need a vacation! I suppose the good news is that we're not alone. Regardless of what business or job we have, each of us can recount examples of stress and tension in our lives.

The better news is we can change the status quo. We can convert stressful situations into situations that are manageable — and we can do it through humor. One example is if you're feeling tense or somewhat stressed due to heavy concentration on meeting a deadline, or trying to analyze a difficult problem, just stop — that's right, STOP. Now relax, take some deep breaths, think of something pleasant in your life — a young child you love to hug or watch, a loved one you enjoy spending time with, or a funny incident that happened recently or a long time ago. This action changes your mood instantly. You start to smile, even laugh, and you are now *in humor*. Humor is that which causes us to smile or laugh, or to be amused. *You cannot be relaxed and smiling, and be tense or stressed at the same time.*

Humor heals illness

Humor releases endorphins, those pain-killing chemicals that are ready to go to work for us whenever we need them. In the middle 1960's, Norman Cousins, the humanitarian and author, wrote the best-seller book, *Anatomy of an Illness*. The book was about his struggle with a debilitating bone disease, and how he survived it despite being given only six months to live. While in the hospital, Cousins, who had a high regard for a positive attitude and for the healing power of humor, asked his doctor to bring him some comedy tapes, such as "The Lucy Show," "Candid Camera," and "The Marx Brothers." He literally laughed himself back to good health — and he lived for another twenty-five years! In his book he wrote that ten minutes of belly laughter is equivalent to two hours of pain-free and restful sleep.

Humor stimulates creativity

Studies have shown that while you're laughing, or immediately after you've been laughing, the mind is at its most creative, and is more effective at solving problems and developing new ideas. That's because the mind is in "open mode" and is more receptive to new concepts and different approaches.

Years ago in London I worked under one of my favorite bosses, who always started a meeting or an interview with light humor. Later he told me that it was the greatest lesson he learned in business and in managing people. It certainly worked, and he was one of the most respected leaders in the large company I worked for. His group came up with some revolutionary ideas, some of which became the foundation of the company's great success. His people were open to learning like children are. Remember how creative we were when we were young children. Our imagination ran wild, with no limitations, and nothing was inconceivable.

A great tool for creative brainstorming is the flip chart where you write every idea that comes up. The trick is not to be judgmental about wild or crazy suggestions: they are what lead to the best creations. And of course they also cause laughter, which in turn keeps creative juices flowing.

Use the following questions to stimulate out-of-the-box ideas, "What if?" and "Why not?" You'll see great things develop.

RECAP

1. Humor aids in learning and memory.
2. Humor builds rapport.
3. Humor reduces tension and stress.
4. Humor heals illness.
5. Humor stimulates creativity

Application Exercise

Write down:

1. What are some areas of your business or job that would benefit by humor?
2. What humorous props or activities will you use to stimulate good rapport and creativity among your employees and coworkers?
3. How will you adjust your training style and format to speed up learning and retention?
5. How will you use humor to start your next meeting?
6. DO IT NOW!

CHAPTER

11

E
EARN RESPECT

We judge ourselves mostly by our intentions,
but others judge us mostly by our actions.
— ERIC HARVEY AND ALEXANDER
LUCIA IN "WALK THE TALK"

In the workplace, one of the biggest complaints I hear from employees at all levels is that they don't get the respect they deserve. Rodney Dangerfield, the stand-up comedian, made a whole career out of the phrase, "I don't get no respect." There was a bestseller song, sung by Aretha Franklin, called "R.E.S.P.E C.T." What constitutes respect? Why must we all have respect?

To be respected can mean being held in high esteem, being admired, even revered; but the common characteristic of respect is being valued by others for what you do and for what you are.

If you manage or supervise other people, their performance is influenced by the degree to which they respect you. They want to know that you are fair, honest, that you keep your word, that you genuinely care about their success, and that you trust them. Miss out on any of those factors and you're begging for trouble and poor employee performance. Work on maintaining those standards and the rewards are unending. Life runs a lot more smoothly, and you'll get a reputation for developing great team players.

How do you earn respect from others?
1. Keep your word.
2. Treat everyone fairly.
3. Demonstrate integrity.
4. Be decisive.

Keep your word

It's obvious that in order to be respected, you need to keep your word, but somehow in this hectic age, many of us fail miserably in this area. Whether it's not keeping a simple promise to meet someone at a certain place and time, or failing to call back with information you promised to get for another person, we all can think of times when we haven't come through with our promises.

I have on more than a half dozen occasions in the last couple of years stopped doing business — or curtailed the amount of business I was conducting with people who cannot keep their word. I have equally stopped calling friends for a lunch or a game of racquetball who are generally unreliable about turning up or about calling back when they said they would.

There's no question that in today's hurly-burly world, where we have so many distractions, and are overwhelmed with information bombarding us from all sides, that we occasionally forget to write something in the calendar or planner, or we lose track of time. We have to discipline ourselves to make an extra effort to live up to our word — just out of simple consideration and respect for others.

It does definitely require a touch of class. In the course of my business, I have occasion to interview many employees, from production-line worker all the way to CEO, and one common complaint heard at all levels is: "You just can't rely on so-and-so to keep his word," or "Oh, of course she said she'd take care of it, she always says that just to get rid of you."

I believe that if we put just a little more effort into living and acting by our word, many of the problems we have will go away, and we will gain a respect from others that we have not enjoyed in the past.

Treat everyone fairly

Most of us believe that we do treat everyone fairly, particularly those of us who manage or supervise other people. The sad part is that when you talk to those who believe they are not treated fairly, many times their argument is very clear. Of course they see their treatment by you from their perspective, while you see it from your perspective.

And therein often lies the problem. I interviewed a customer support operator in a manufacturing plant, and she told me that some of the sales reps "treat us like dirt." When I asked her to explain, she told me that often they call her on the phone while they are with a client, and berate her for her failure to make something happen that was affecting the client's satisfaction, such as a late delivery. In many cases the failure to deliver was out of her control, but the salesperson, she believed, wanted to give the client the impression that he was tough, and that he was taking charge of the problem immediately. When I examined the salesperson's perspective, I found, not untypically, that there was a misunderstanding of how problems like this occurred, how to correct them in the future, and how to prevent them. The salesperson saw a lack of urgency, whereas there was really a lack of communication. And the result was a lack of respect for those in the sales department because they took out their frustrations on less resourceful employees who also had less authority.

Demonstrate integrity

> *If leaders are careless about basic things — telling the truth, respecting moral codes, proper professional conduct — who can believe them on other issues?*
>
> —James L. Hayes

By integrity I mean honesty, openness, honor, principled. We might think of certain people or companies who stand out — such as Johnson and Johnson several years ago when someone infected some Tylenol and the company executives insisted on removing millions of dollars worth of the medicine from shelves everywhere — risking bankruptcy. You most likely have worked with a boss or a colleague at some time whose integrity, or lack of it, still stands out among her faults or weaknesses.

We sometimes ask, what's the honorable thing to do? If you find a $100 bill on the floor near the water cooler in your office building, isn't there just the smallest temptation to keep it and say nothing about it? Integrity is making an effort to get it back to the person who lost it. Another example is claiming glory for yourself as a result of the achievements of another — which is not the practice of integrity. Nor is blaming others for your mistakes.

Be sensitive and considerate

It seems alien for some people to be sensitive. I think many women are more sensitive than men. Some women, when asked about what they like in a man, usually say he should be sensitive and considerate. What kind of sensitivity are we talking about?

Being sensitive involves courtesy, good manners, good taste, a touch of class, a feeling for others' interests and concerns. If you are a manager, do your employees feel that you are interested in their well being, that you care about their problems or difficulties? If they do, then they will be loyal to you.

What about sensitivity in public? When you're having dinner with your friend or family, or a client, and your cell phone rings, do you pick it up and launch into a loud conversation in front of them without excusing yourself or moving away to a quiet area? I have gently admonished one or two of my friends for such behavior, though I realize it was not their intention to offend. Some people are quite surprised to be thought of as rude or insensitive. Perhaps the good habit of public courtesy should be taught in school: unlike algebra, it has permanent applicability to all of us, and it would surely enhance our human skills.

RECAP

1. Keep your word.
2. Treat everyone fairly.
3. Demonstrate integrity.
4. Be sensitive and considerate.

Application Exercise

Write down:

1. What are some opportunities you have to break your word?
2. What are one or two occasions when you have unwittingly treated someone unfairly?
3. What good examples of integrity can you bring to mind and share with those you teach or manage?
4. How will you apply these principles?
5. DO IT NOW!

<u>E</u>

EXPECT TO

SUCCEED

When you only set out to do what you already know you can do, you never develop a true sense of confidence.

— BARBARA DE ANGELIS

In the second chapter I talked about changing your expectations. Here we expand on that, but in the sense of our vision of the future. Do you expect to succeed, to fail, or maybe just to get by? Maybe you're hoping that all will work out for the best, as most people do. I used to think like that, but I found that desired success comes with a conviction — a belief that what you want to become is indeed possible. I learned that developing a mindset, an attitude, of success and accomplishment almost makes it *natural* for us to advance and succeed.

I watched successful people whom I admired, and I noticed one common thread: they all anticipated success despite the apparent obstacles. Of course they also took action to make it happen.

How can you develop this mindset to anticipate success — to expect to succeed?

1. Affirm your achievements in advance.
2. Take action.
3. Hang around success-talking people.
4. Start a Victory File.

Affirm your achievements in advance

It starts when you get up in the morning and it continues when you go to bed. That's right. As soon as we wake up and get ready for the day, we are getting ready for a good day, a bad day, or a mediocre day. We do that by how we talk to ourselves. We talk to ourselves all the time, almost every minute of every day. And what we say becomes a directive to our system — our subconscious, our computer — on what it should do with us today.

For example, the positive self-talk person, upon waking in the morning, will say "Good morning, God." The negative person will say "Good God, it's morning!" Just a few years ago I started saying, upon waking, "This is going to be a great day." I should tell you that at first I wasn't convinced, but by making it a habit, it became a normal way to get up, and my day definitely went better than when I woke up and just *hoped* for a good day. It's not that you're suddenly and magically going to create fantastic experiences on this day, but it does set you up to take charge of how you want your day to go; it also helps you *respond* to different and tough situations rather than just *reacting.*

William James, the American psychologist said, "You are what you think about most of the time." Many of us go around all our lives affirming failure, "I'm no good with people," "I could never get up to speak in front of a crowd," "I always get upset when people complain."

Our actions and feelings mirror our thoughts. We can reverse those negative self-talk habits by saying the opposite, such as "I am getting much better at dealing with difficult people," "I am becoming more comfortable speaking in front of a group," "I have become more confident and patient when responding to complaints."

Visualize success

Some of the great inventors, entrepreneurs, architects, artists, and philanthropists, were great visionaries. They could *see* what they wanted to create, and they could *experience* the results of what they planned to do, to make, or to build. We can learn to do that too. It's one of the great success tools.

In my second year of speaking, I was offered an engagement in Nassau, Bahamas — to speak to 800 people. Naturally I was excited, but later I realized I was now quite scared. The largest group I had spoken to up till then was 145 people, and my average-size audience for the seminars I presented was around 50. The thought of speaking to 800 people — in another country, with a different culture was exciting and terrifying at the same time. While I knew that this was an opportunity of a lifetime and a chance to rise to a new dimension of accomplishment, I had butterflies in my stomach just thinking about it.

Around the time I got the booking, the "Success Lectures" were coming to my city, and one of the speakers was my favorite, Zig Ziglar, who headed up a group of four of the top speakers in the country, along with a couple of celebrity speakers. I thought this was timely. I could get some fresh inspiration while watching the masters in action, and pick up some tips to prepare for my big challenge. So I bought a ticket for a seat in the front section, close to the stage. Zig was the second speaker on, and the main draw. After his great one-hour motivational presentation and the rousing applause, he went off the stage and the emcee announced a twenty-minute break so the attendees could refresh and buy tapes and books — many supplied by Zig, who also signed autographs.

Right at this time, as people slowly moved from their seats, I got an idea. I already knew that there were about 5,000 people in the auditorium. I wanted to get a feel for what it would be like to stand on stage in front of such a crowd. Without much thinking I went to the side of the stage and slowly climbed the steps. I stood — a bit awkwardly — and looked out over the crowd, all the way from the lower seats way up into the balcony. I slowly walked across the stage, a bit nervous as I felt people looking at me, probably wondering who I was and why I wasn't announced. Some people who were leaving their seats actually sat down again. I felt a strange power being up there, feeling that if I had a microphone everyone watching would listen.

This now became my vision. I had three weeks before my trip to Nassau, and every night before going to sleep, I pictured myself on stage presenting to 5,000 people. I was articulate, knowledgeable, remembering my lines, sharing some great quotations and funny stories. I saw my audience nodding their heads, smiling, laughing and applauding. As I practiced my speech during the day I found my confidence building up. I was ready to speak from a big stage to 5,000 people. Yes, now you've guessed it. When I went to Nassau and took the platform in front of 800 people, it was as if I had done it before in front of a much larger audience. What a great difference the visualization had made to my confidence and my performance!

Take action

> *Nothing happens until something moves.*
> —Albert Einstein

When I first read books on positive thinking back in my thirties, I thought that all I had to do was dream and visualize the result I wanted, and presto, there it was. Not so, as we all find out sooner or later.

Even now I have a good friend who reads all the books on motivation, about understanding yourself, living your dream, and conquering fear. He gets really impressed and excited by a great motivational speaker, and yet over these past few years, he has rarely taken any kind of risk or even made any significant change in pursuing a better life. He expects it to happen based on occasional self-talk and some wishful thinking, without taking any action himself, and then feels guilty he's made little progress. George Bernard said, "Regret for the things we did can be tempered by time; it is regret for the things we did not do that is inconsolable."

Self-talk is an aid to, not a substitute for, action. For me, an Irishman, it's like bread and butter. I don't like bread without butter; by the same token, I would not eat butter on its own. Neither of these foods on their own would accomplish the same result or enjoyment I want to gain from bread and butter. The butter is an aid, or an add-on, and not a substitute.

In sports, many athletes and sports stars practice visualization and positive affirmation, but they also get out there and practice much more than those who might be considered average. They know that they have to get the mind and body working together to achieve the great goals they've set for themselves.

Hang around success-talking people

Isn't it amazing how the company we keep, especially when we're younger, affects us. If you're easily influenced by others, it would behoove you to spend as much of your "buddy" time with those friends or acquaintances whom you see as positive and upbeat, and abandon the whiners and complainers unless you can get them to change their ways, which is highly unlikely!

Sometimes it's tough to know whom to avoid at first. Have you ever gone to a convention and sat next to someone who was totally negative? He was there only because his boss sent him — probably to change his attitude! It's hard to change these people no matter how hard you try. After a while you can become adept at spotting a more positive acquaintance or fellow attendee and say, "Oh, there's Bill. I need to catch him. I'll see you later."

Start a victory file

One of the greatest tools for moving to a higher level of achievement is to acknowledge and brag on what you've accomplished before. The benefit of doing this is that it refreshes your mind about what is possible. We so easily forget what great things we've done in the past — those achievements that can often lend inspiration to the challenges we face in the present.

In the job arena, this is particularly true if you're in line for the annual job review or appraisal. How intimidating those can be, especially if you haven't prepared with a list of all your successes in the recent year — those successes which easily justify your importance to the company and provide you with necessary ammunition to negotiate a well-deserved raise.

I started my Victory File, my success file, a few years ago when I began my speaking and training business; and almost immediately after I started using it, I noticed a new enthusiasm and confidence as I tackled some of the challenges I was facing. I listed every achievement I could think of. Obviously I couldn't recall them all in one sitting, but I set my mind to try to remember. I went back as far as I could to find any kind of accomplishment that I was proud of — even those, which at the time didn't seem significant. I remembered disarming a bully in the orphanage by doing comical impersonations of one of our teachers. I now realized that this was indeed a *victory*.

I'll bet you can find a ton of successes in your life — such as winning at a swim meet, getting appointed to a prestigious committee, getting a promotion, climbing a mountain, speaking to a small group for the first time and surviving it, coming in under a tough budget, closing a major deal, seeing your children graduate, getting your article printed in the company newsletter, giving up smoking, losing ten pounds, and so on.

As I fill out this Victory File, I place an asterisk next to any achievement I had which at the time I didn't think

I could do, or was even terrified of trying, like the Nassau speech. So now, when I am facing a little uncertainty or fear about an upcoming challenge, I simply pull out my Victory File and realize that what I'm worried about pales in comparison to what I have already faced and accomplished in my life.

RECAP
1. Affirm your achievements in advance.
2. Take action.
3. Hang around success-talking people.
4. Start a Victory File.

Application Exercise

Write down:
1. List a few things you'd like to accomplish, perhaps a higher paying job, a special dream house or car, a trip to China, or a better relationship with your boss, your child, or your spouse.
2. How would you act if you achieved any one of these? For example, you might walk tall, dress more stylishly, communicate with great confidence, and share your success with another person.
3. When will you begin visualizing these outcomes and begin expecting to succeed? Put down a date — like today!
4. DO IT NOW!

CHAPTER

13

P
PROMOTE SUCCESS IN OTHERS

"You can have anything in life you want if you'll just help enough other people get what they want."

— ZIG ZIGLAR

How true are those words of Zig Ziglar, who has certainly helped a lot of people with his words and his wisdom. To promote success in others is simply to reach out and help people in any way: help them advance, help them understand, help them cope with difficulties, help them succeed.

We are all coaches in some way when it comes to influencing growth and achievement in others, whether they are our children, our spouses, or our employees. What nobler way to show appreciation for your own blessings and success than to help others to do the same.

What are some ways you can promote success in others?

1. Make a decision, as part of your way of life, to help others succeed.
2. Identify those who have a desire to grow and help them.
3. Give of your time and your resources.
4. Celebrate their successes.

Make a decision as part of your way of life to help others

Most of us are not programmed to help others as a planned part of our life, like going to work or having three meals a day. And that's why we often miss out on the greatest activity of all — giving and contributing to others. We do it when the occasion arises, such as when a catastrophe occurs we send cash, or we volunteer in some way to help alleviate suffering or loss. And that is very commendable.

But when we consciously make this a way of life, then we are totally enriched and, magically, less burdened with our own imagined problems.

Identify those who have a desire to grow — and help them

I have found that there are some people in life who just don't want to be helped. They would rather steep in self-pity and attention-seeking whining than to get up and do something to change their lives. Happily they are in the minority, but you shouldn't waste time on them unless you're a genius at transforming committed losers.

Conversely, there are many individuals out there with a quiet dedication to service and responsibility, but who need your help and guidance to move them up a notch or two. Not all of them have the courage to ask for help.

Not all of them are outgoing enough for you to spot them. But they are there, and you'd be amazed at the power of at least a word of encouragement. One day, coming through the checkout at my local food store I told the cashier, Yolanda, that she was my favorite checkout person because she always made me feel good with her cheerful smile and good eye contact. She beamed and said, "Why, thank you, sir; nobody ever said anything like that to me before."

Did that incident fit into the principle of promoting success in others? I believe it did. After all, is success not about feeling good about what you're doing? And are you not sometimes motivated by other people's appreciation of your performance?

Give of your time and your resources

A lot has been written about *giving*, the giving of money, of your time, or your expertise. Then there's that great phrase, initiated no doubt by a giver or philanthropist, which says, "What goes around comes around." We can all think of some experiences to validate this truth, whether we were the receiver or the giver of a kindness of some kind.

Many years ago when I was a corporate department manager and still ascending the career ladder, I spotted a young management trainee in one of our hotels in London who impressed me as being a go-getter and a willing and enthusiastic person. Each time I saw him in action, he looked as if he was having a good time. I spoke with him occasionally, only to find that he was a bit frustrated in not being able to have more input in how things were done and how service could be improved.

I had him assigned to a committee that gave him more exposure to other company executives. I also let him work with my assistant for a day to see how the corporate office functioned and how we communicated with the hotels in the field. When a more senior assistant manager's position became vacant, I recommended David as a candidate. He got the job and over a period of six months I saw him do great things. He reduced turnover, and he got his employees much more involved in making positive changes. As I watched him do great things, I felt proud that I had discovered him and that I was able to help him advance.

Many years later, after I had been in the United States working for a consulting company, and later managing a group of hotels, I lost my job through a takeover. I sent my resume out to all the big hotel chains and management companies. One day the phone rang in my house in Virginia where I lived at the time. It was a Welsh accent, and the person calling was my old protégé from over fifteen years ago.

David was now the vice president for human resources for an international hotel chain, headquartered in London. My resume, which I had sent to the American office of the company in New York, had landed on his desk in London, among the hundreds he received weekly. He remembered my name and called me almost immediately.

After some discussions he decided that his company might be able to use my consulting expertise in their European hotels. This began a series of trips to London and Amsterdam where I completed several projects in the company's more prestigious hotels. This was a lot better than being out of work! At the end of my agreement with David and the European operations, I was offered a job running hotels once again, back in the United States.

Another example of how we gain in different ways by promoting success in others is the Teddy story.

The Teddy Story

Many years ago there was an elementary school teacher, whose name was Mrs. Thompson. As she stood in front of her fifth-grade class the first day of school, she told the children a lie. Like most teachers she looked at her students and said that she loved them all the same; but that was impossible because there in the front row, slumped in his seat, was a little boy named Teddy Stoddard.

Mrs. Thompson had watched Teddy the year before and noticed that he didn't play well with the other children, that his clothes were messy, and that he constantly needed a bath.

Teddy could be unpleasant. It got to the point where Mrs. Thompson would actually take delight in marking his papers with a broad red pen, making bold Xs, and putting a big F at the top of his paper.

At the school where Mrs. Thompson taught, she was required to review each child's past records, and she put Teddy's off until last. However, when she reviewed his file she was in for a surprise. Teddy's first grade teacher wrote, "Teddy is a bright child with a ready laugh. He does his work neatly and he has good manners. He's a joy to be around."

His second-grade teacher wrote, "Teddy is an excellent student, well liked by his classmates, but he's troubled because his mother has a terminal illness, and life at home must be a struggle."

His third-grade teacher wrote, "His mother's death has been hard on him; he tries to do his best, but his father doesn't show much interest, and his home life will soon affect him if steps aren't taken."

Teddy's fourth-grade teacher wrote, "Teddy's withdrawn and doesn't show much interest at school. He doesn't have many friends and sometimes he even sleeps in class."

By now Mrs. Thompson realized the problem and she was ashamed of herself. She felt even worse when her students brought her Christmas presents wrapped in beautiful ribbon and bright paper — except for Teddy. His present was clumsily wrapped in heavy brown paper he'd gotten from the grocery bag. Mrs. Thompson took pains to open it in the middle of the other presents.

Some of the children started to laugh when she found a rhinestone bracelet with some of the stones missing and a bottle that was one quarter full of perfume. But she stifled the children's laughter when she explained how pretty the bracelet was, putting it on and dabbing some of the perfume on her wrist.

Teddy Stoddard stayed after school that day, just long enough to say, " Mrs. Thompson, today you smell just like my mom used to." After the children left she cried for at least an hour. On that very day she quit teaching reading, writing, and arithmetic, and instead she began to teach children. Mrs. Thompson paid particular attention to Teddy as she worked with him, and his mind seemed to come alive. The more she encouraged, the faster he responded. By the end of the year, Teddy had become one of the smartest children in the class, and despite her lie, became one of *her* teacher's pets.

A year later she found a note under the door from Teddy, telling her that she was still the best teacher he ever had in his whole life.

Six years went by before she got another note from Teddy. He then wrote that he had finished high school, third in his class — and she was still the best teacher he ever had in his whole life.

Four years after that she got another letter saying that while things have been tough at times, he stayed in school and stuck with it and would soon graduate from college with the highest of honors. He assured Mrs. Thompson that she was still the very best and favorite teacher he ever had in his whole life.

Then four more years passed and yet another letter came. This time he explained that after he got his bachelor's degree, he decided to go a little further. The letter said that she was still the best and favorite teacher had. But now his name was a little longer. The letter was signed "Theodore F. Stoddard, MD."

But the story doesn't end there; you see there was another letter that spring. Teddy said he met this girl and was going to be married. He explained that his father had died a couple of years ago and he was wondering if Mrs. Thompson might agree to sit in the place at the wedding that was usually reserved for the mother of the groom. Of course Mrs. Thompson did. And guess what, she wore that bracelet, the one with several rhinestones missing and she made sure she was wearing the perfume that Teddy remembered his mother wearing on their last Christmas together.

They hugged each other, and Dr. Stoddard whispered in Mrs. Thompson's ear, "Thank you so much for making me feel important and showing me that I could make a difference." Mrs. Thompson, with tears in her eyes, said, "Teddy, you have it all wrong. You were the one who taught me that I could make a difference. I didn't know how to teach till I had met you."

I am a strong believer that we can best promote additional success in others by volunteerism, giving our time. In business, this might mean spending some extra time with an employee outside of your own work schedule. The icing on the cake is that for you, the volunteer, there is no greater reward than to see the smile, the progress, and the pride of the person you helped. You'll notice that you are not as stressed as you used to be. You seem to have fewer worries because by helping others you lose some of the problems you thought you had.

Celebrate their successes

To be happy about the achievements and successes of those whom you lead or develop is to be a leader who sees their accomplishments as a part of your own success. There are times when we are a little jealous of those who enjoy success, especially if we aren't having a winning day or week. But there is no reason to miss out on the thrill of seeing those you've mentored or coached do well.

You should take it personally. You share in that responsibility. You were part of the winning team. You helped make a difference in that person's life. What a great therapy that is. Just knowing that you used your power to influence some little success in anyone is indeed a great self-booster.

And the other, even greater, benefit is that when you celebrate other people's success with them, they will be motivated to excel even further. So it's a great management tool also. I had a manager work for me once. Sharon was a class act when it came to celebrating her employees' successes. She also knew well that some of her new hires were slower to learn some of the systems, such as the computer, and that they needed even more encouragement than most.

Every month she had a staff meeting of her twenty employees, and she handed out the paychecks at the same time. She used this meeting — knowing everyone would be there — to publicly recognize employees who had made any kind of visible progress, as well as those who had demonstrated efforts outside of the norm. Each one received applause from his or her colleagues. They were also encouraged to find a compliment to make about any other employee who had either done something special, who had helped them in some way, or who was just a great team player and fun to work with.

The results of this philosophy of celebrating co-workers' successes were that the operation flourished, with very little turnover. Customers loved the service consistency delivered by employees they knew, and there was a strong sense of camaraderie among team members.

I have a literacy student, Steven, whom I tutor once a week. In the beginning he was somewhat shy and intimidated by all the things he didn't know. As we connected the lessons to some application in his work as stock clerk in a retail store, we started to make exciting progress. He told me when I first met him and asked him how being able to read and write better would help him, that often he needed to write down hand-over notes to the supervisor on the next shift. But he couldn't spell well or assemble a sentence correctly, so after he was criticized once for a "confusing" message, he gave up writing any notes.

Just imagine my excitement when after about our third session he sent his first short note to his next shift co-worker. He was proud, as was I. At the same time he started a Victory File. He bought himself a spiral-bound notebook and eagerly entered his accomplishments; not just his literacy improvements, but also his other activities. For instance he's a runner and also a cyclist, so he's constantly tracking his time and trying to beat previous records. These scores now went into his Victory File, and we celebrate and talk-up his achievements each time we get together. I feel great every time I leave our meetings, knowing that he has advanced a little more once again.

Last year he obtained his first computer, which was a huge ordeal for him. Our tutoring shifted to getting him started on the basics. Up till now he was getting practice at hand-writing letters to his sister and to a couple of friends in other states. Now he can type those letters. We've also been working on e-mail and the Internet. We now e-mail each other to confirm our appointments. This is another source of celebration as he shares with me e-mails he's had from friends and relatives, who before this couldn't even imagine Steve owning a computer.

RECAP

1. Make a decision as part of your way of life to help others succeed.
2. Identify those who have a desire to grow and help them.
3. Give of your time and your resources.
4. Celebrate their successes.

Application Exercise

Write down:

1. Compose a list of anyone at work or at home, or any entity or organization, including a charity, that you would like to help right now.
2. Select at least one that you now intend to help in some way.
3. Decide on a minimum amount of time you will reserve for this aspect of your life's program, an hour a week, two days a month, etc.
4. DO IT NOW!

CHAPTER 14

HOW TO APPLY THESE PRINCIPLES DAILY

Success is nothing more than a few simple disciplines, practiced every day; while failure is simply a few errors in judgment, repeated every day. It is the accumulative weight of our disciplines and our judgments that leads us to either fortune or failure.

— JIM ROHN

A s with any seminar you've attended or book you've read or instruction you've received, there is no benefit unless you use the information or training to improve your situation in some way, to expand your horizons, or to move to the next level of knowledge or competence.

Many people fail to act on newly acquired information because it requires them to change their habits in some way. And our habits keep us comfortable and secure. Even though we know and believe that what we just learned will be of great benefit to us, we subconsciously sabotage our success by finding excuses not to get started on this new behavioral change.

How can you gain the benefits from the lessons learned as soon as possible?
1. Ask the "Three Questions."
2. Start in small ways at first.
3. Write a daily "To Do" list.
4. Tell others of your success.
5. Start applying one of the principles.

Ask the "Three Questions"

I learned this technique from one of my favorite bosses. These three powerful questions will revolutionize your way of communicating with your employees, your clients, and even with yourself. They will improve your leadership abilities and they will make your meetings more productive. They are:
- What's going well?
- What could go better?
- What do we need to do to make things go even better?

Take the first question, "What's going well?" Make a point to start every meeting in the future with this question. Isn't it obvious how this question can help you establish an air of enthusiasm about the good things — or good news in your company? Too often we dwell on the problems, trying to allocate blame and ending in conflict. Get people to tell you what they feel good about today. Do the same for yourself. Anything positive is worth mentioning. Someone closed a new deal or picked up a new client; someone was promoted; a colleague announced a baby on the way; someone's interview was published in the local media.

The second question, "What could go better?" helps you, in a collaborative manner, to determine what problems need to be tackled, and what potential improvement can be identified — without pointing accusatory fingers at others, or at other departments who may be deficient in some areas. This approach has a positive impact and it leads to expeditious problem solving.

The third question, "What do we need to do to make things go even better?" is a logical follow-up on the previous two questions. You have already set the positive tone, and your mind is now in the open mode, flexible and curious to others' ideas.

Start in small ways at first

We all know how difficult we sometimes find it to get started on a project. Part of the problem is that we see the project as a bigger challenge than it really is. I was thinking like that when I had the idea to write this book. It seemed so enormous that my mind went blank, or I became tense every time I thought about starting.

When I finally sat down and did an outline — actually a mind map — of all the headings and ideas that I wanted to incorporate, then I started a roll. Then, by breaking it down into single ideas, then single sentences, I began to make progress. I now aim for 1000 words in a day. Sometimes I write more, sometimes less.

Apply that thinking — a little every day — to whatever problem or project you have to handle, and your chances of progress will improve greatly. If you were going to paint the inside of the house, one action would be to write down the measurements to determine how much paint to buy. Buying the paint is another action. Trying to do everything all at once is what causes us to put it off.

Write your daily "To Do" list

Be proactive as you were in chapter four. If you don't have a written list of what you have to do, the important things definitely won't get done. That was my biggest failing when I started my own business. Now I write a list every evening. Actually it's a running "To Do" list that I just update every day onto a new list. I do mine on real paper. You may have some computer system that works better for you.

Part of the efficiency of a "To Do" list is that it gets you focused. You can see at a glance what you have to do, and therefore you can special-mark your priorities with a circle or a red mark to highlight them. Then you can decide which item (shoot for the toughest) you'll get started on next morning. Put everything related to that task on your desk, ready for action.

Make a big line through each item or part of a task when you've completed it. This is very satisfying and it makes you feel as if you are accomplishing great things.

Tell others of your success

There's nothing wrong with a little bragging. And the validation you get from true friends and those who care about your success will boost your efforts and your confidence to persevere — whether you're building a patio, writing a book, quitting smoking, or running a political campaign. They'll also be asking you how the project is coming along which gives you that sense of accountability you were trying to find!

Start applying one of the principles

The measure of a valuable lesson is how you apply it to your life — how you use it to accomplish a task, meet a challenge, or solve a problem. We have thirteen principles here, and any single one of them may be called upon to assist you at any time, on any day, in any circumstance you encounter.

Imagine you have a problem, and that you are very frustrated in not being able to solve it despite your efforts over many months. Using these principles, which one will you call to mind? How about "Look for a better way"? You might then consider one of the subheadings of that chapter, such as "look for the second right answer", or "ask what if? or why not?"

Another example is that you're having difficulty dealing with a new job or a new boss. Which principle might help here? How about "Change your expectations"? Maybe you're expecting the unreal; maybe you're assuming too much, and therefore becoming disappointed or angry based on your own expectations. You might consider the sub-heading "reframe the situation."

Try out one of these principles today — NOW, and again tomorrow, and keep applying one or more of them until it becomes a habit, and you're definitely on your way to greater things.

And remember, **LEAP, DON'T SLEEP!**

BIOGRAPHY

John Madden works with companies to eliminate mediocrity in customer service and business practices, and to develop self-motivated employees.

He and his older brother, Eddie, were brought up in an Irish orphanage. When he was twelve, his aunt took them to live with her in her small hotel in Dublin, where she put them to work, while they also attended school.

John went on to manage multiple hotels and restaurants in Europe and in the United States.

He is a member of the National Speakers Association and the American Society for Training and Development. He presents keynotes and seminars on Creative Problem Solving, Coaching Skills, Customer Retention, Interpersonal Skills, and Stress Management through Humor.

John has published articles and recordings on various topics, and is a contributing writer to business journals and the Chamber of Commerce.

Order More Copies of
"Leap Don't Sleep!"

Visit our web site at www.LeapDontSleep.com and enjoy a multiple-copy discount.

Or…Call 316-689-6932, or toll free 1-800-301-2924

Call John at the same number to present after-dinner motivational humor, keynotes and seminars for your conventions, or in-house presentations and workshops on "Leap, Don't Sleep!" and other results-oriented topics for managers and employees.

Additional Tools for Success – by John Madden

Success is a Laughing Matter   Video and Audio
Accelerate your success through laughter and humor.

Look for a Better Way: Audio
How to get dramatically different results by taking different and more creative action.

Change Your Expectations: Audio
How to move from failure thinking to success programming.

Stress Down with Humor: Audio
Manage and control your stress through humor.

Outstanding Customer Service: Audio
How to win a competitive edge through service excellence.

The S.E.R.V.I.C.E. Principles: Audio
How to guarantee repeat customers by implementing the seven principles.

Where Do I Go From Here?   Video
How to get from where you are … to where you want to be.